Imagery of Triumph and Rebellion in 2 Corinthians 2:14-17 and Elsewhere in the Epistle

An Example of the Combination of Greco-Roman and Judaic Traditions in the Apostle Paul

Roger David Aus

Studies in Judaism

University Press of America,® Inc.
Lanham • Boulder • New York • Toronto • Oxford

Copyright © 2005 by
University Press of America,® Inc.
4501 Forbes Boulevard
Suite 200
Lanham, Maryland 20706
UPA Acquisitions Department (301) 459-3366

PO Box 317
Oxford
OX2 9RU, UK

All rights reserved
Printed in the United States of America
British Library Cataloging in Publication Information Available

Library of Congress Control Number: 2005930954

ISBN: 978-0-7618-3321-5

∞™ The paper used in this publication meets the minimum
requirements of American National Standard for Information
Sciences—Permanence of Paper for Printed Library Materials,
ANSI Z39.48—1984

Studies in Judaism

EDITOR

Jacob Neusner
Bard College

EDITORIAL BOARD

Alan J. Avery-Peck
College of the Holy Cross

Herbert Basser
Queens University

Bruce D. Chilton
Bard College

José Faur
Bar Ilan University

William Scott Green
University of Rochester

Mayer Gruber
Ben-Gurion University of the Negev

Günter Stemberger
University of Vienna

James F. Strange
University of South Florida

Dedicated

to

Martin Hengel, who has convincingly taught us not to separate
too readily the "Hellenistic" from the "Judaic,"

and

Christian Wolff, a kind, caring, and conscientious
"Kenner" of Corinthians

Table of Contents

Preface vii
Introduction ix
I. Imagery of Triumph 1
    1. Eternal Triumph 7
    2. Thanksgiving, with Incense 9
        2.1 Preliminary Thanksgiving 9
        2.2 Thanksgivings, Including Incense, at the End of the
            Triumphal Procession 11
    3. The Triumphator and His Officers in the Triumphal
        Procession 16
    4. Centers for the Collection of Money, and the Offerings of
        First-fruits in the Jerusalem Temple 23
    5. Suspicion of Fiscal Impropriety 26
    6. Family Pedigree 29
        6.1 King Perseus 29
        6.2 Paulus 30
    7. Boasting and Weakness 31
    8. Consolation 33
    9. The "Ovatio," and a Triumph Through Persuasion 36
    10. No Triumph for Fighting in Another's Province 39
    11. The Meaning of θριαμβεύω in 2 Cor 2:14-17 40
II. Judaic Imagery of Rebellion 47
    1. The Masoretic Text 50
    2. The Septuagint 52
    3. Wisdom of Solomon 18:20-25 52
    4. Philo of Alexandria 57
    5. 4 Maccabees 7:11 59
    6. The Targums 60
        6.1 Sweet-smelling or Aromatic Incense 60
        6.2 The Destroyer 62
        6.3 Praying 63
        6.4 A Partition 63
    7. Rabbinic Sources 64
        7.1 The Angel of Death 64
        7.2 Prayer 66

   7.3 The Dead and the Living 67
   7.4 Salvation 68
   7.5 Sufficient 70
   7.6 Fragrance and Sweet-smelling Odor 72
  8. 1 Corinthians 10:10 74
Summary 81
Sources and Reference Works 85
Author Index 93
About the Author 95

Preface

Having worked almost exclusively in the Gospels for many years, it has been very refreshing for me now to return to the Pauline Corpus, in which I started my New Testament work at Yale University in 1971 with the dissertation *Comfort in Judgment. The Use of Day of the Lord and Theophany Traditions in 2 Thessalonians 1*. (I would still argue that the Pauline authorship of this writing should at least remain an open question.) I took early retirement as a pastor a year and a half ago, in part so that my own congregation could merge with its neighbor and "mother" church, and survive financially. Finally, I now had enough free time to spend several months reading original and secondary sources connected to the triumph of a Roman general, who returned successfully from a major battle and conducted a triumphal procession through Rome, in the "Institut für Klassische Philologie" at Berlin's Free University. My thanks go to the friendly library staff and students there, who accepted me as one of their own for so long.

Wayne Meeks of Yale University graciously provided me with a copy of his student Regina Plunkett-Dowling's 2001 dissertation, *Reading and Restoration: Paul's Use of Scripture in 2 Corinthians 1–9*. Martha Lund Smalley of the Yale Divinity School Library staff generously photocopied several articles and excerpts from volumes unavailable to me in Berlin. The theological library of the Humboldt University here again provided its usual kind assistance, and Cilliers Breytenbach, head of the "Institut für Urchristentum und Antike" at the theological faculty, and who himself has written on the triumph, kindly called my attention to several pieces of relevant secondary literature. Dieter Zeller of Mainz and John Fitzgerald of the University of Miami critically read the manuscript and made several helpful suggestions, especially in regard to Part I, and Niko Oswald of the "Institut für Judaistik" of the Free University in Berlin did the same, especially in regard to Part II. The Rev. Dr. Thomas Day aided me in the proofreading. My son Jonathan again took time off his own doctoral work in Oslo and formatted the manuscript. To them all my heartfelt thanks.

Professor Jacob Neusner graciously accepted this study for his series "Studies in Judaism." The Pharisaic Jew Saul, born in the Greek-speaking city of Tarsus of Cilicia, according to Acts studied in Jerusalem (in Hebrew, or possibly Aramaic) with Gamaliel (I) and was "educated strictly according to our ancestral law, being zealous for God" (22:3; cf. 5:34 and Gal 1:14). Having first severely persecuted the messianic sect of Christians ("the Way"), after his conversion to Christianity Paul just as zealously as before now missionized throughout the eastern Mediterranean area, even hoping to go to Spain, in Judaic sources thought to be the end of the world. In his letters, all in Greek, this bilingual Jewish Christian reveals extensive knowledge of both Greco-Roman and Judaic traditions, the latter in Greek, Hebrew and Aramaic. An excellent example of such knowledge is found in 2 Cor 2:14-17, which employs Greco-Roman imagery of the triumph, as well as Judaic traditions of rebellion in Num 17:6-15 (Eng. 16:41-50). In this respect the following study appropriately fits this series.

The standard abbreviations are employed throughout the investigation. The textual editions are described more fully in "Sources and Reference Works" at the end of the volume so that the reader can look up the passages cited and form his or her own opinion about them. An author index is included, especially to indicate where I differ from other major interpreters.

The positive results of this study surprised me too. That is what is fascinating in "New" Testament research when one deals with the original sources while asking relevant questions in a new way. I hope the reader, whether Christian or Jew, will share my enthusiasm.

Roger David Aus
Pentecost 2005
Berlin, Germany

Introduction

Second Corinthians is one of the most demanding writings for the interpreter of Paul, in part because 2:13, ending with "Macedonia," would logically seem to be best followed by 7:5, which begins with "Macedonia." The unit 2:14-17 begins a section dealing with the Apostle's ministry, including reconciliation. It concludes at 6:13, followed by 7:2-4. Or, if 6:14 - 7:1 are a digression by Paul, they are also to be included in the larger section of 2:14 - 7:14.[1]

In this study I will focus on two types of imagery found in 2:14-17,[2] first that of "triumph" in part I, and secondly that of "rebellion" in part II. Basically, the first deals with Greco-Roman, and the second with Judaic sources. My analysis will address questions such as the connection of 2:13 to 14;[3] why a thanksgiving occurs in v 14; the meaning of "always," θριαμβεύω, "us," "in every place," and "fragrance" in v 14; "aroma" and "those who are being saved" and "those who are perishing" in v 15; and "a fragrance from death to death" and "a fragrance from life to life," as well as the adjective "sufficient" in v 16. A Summary gathers the results of the two parts and applies them to the pericope.

---

[1] On the various partition theories for this epistle, cf. the standard commentaries. While not necessarily favoring the present order of the chapters, I consider them all to be from Paul and to belong to the Corinthian correspondence after First Corinthians. Therefore I quote from all sections in this study.

[2] My analysis does not deal as extensively with v 17, yet it belongs to the unit.

[3] Cf. Regina Plunkett-Dowling, *Reading and Restoration: Paul's Use of Scripture in 2 Corinthians 1-9* (2001 Yale Ph.D. dissertation) 2 : "the sudden, unexplained shift from travel itinerary to elevated metaphor at 2:14...." Hans Dieter Betz considers 2 Cor 1:1-2:13 to be part of the so-called "letter of reconciliation," and 2:14-6:13 together with 7:24 to be a fragment, "part of an apology." See his *2 Corinthians 8 and 9* (Hermeneia; Philadelphia: Fortress, 1985) 142-43. Joachim Kügler, "Paulus und der Duft des triumphierenden Christus. Zum kulturellen Basisbild von 2 Kor 2,14-16," in *Von Jesus zum Christus*. Festschrift Paul Hoffmann, ed. Rudolf Hoppe and Ulrich Busse (BZNW 93; Berlin: de Gruyter, 1998) 157 also thinks 2:13 to 14 is a "thematic leap," the latter verse beginning "the fragment of another text."

I. Imagery of Triumph

2 Cor 2:14 reads in the NRSV: "But thanks be to God, who in Christ always 'leads us in triumphal procession'...." The present active participle θριαμβεύοντι here derives from θριαμβεύω, which has the basic meaning of "to triumph," "to lead in triumph."[1] Just as the Roman citizen Paul[2] employed in his letters imagery from athletic contests, for example the Isthmian Games held near Corinth,[3] so he utilizes here a Greek expression which characterized the Roman triumph. The Apostle was most probably also aware of the recent triumphs celebrated in Rome by Germanicus Caesar in 17 CE,[4] Caligula in 40 CE,[5] and by

---

[1] Cf. LSJ 806; BAGD 363; Lampe, *A Patristic Lexicon* 654-55; art. θριαμβεύω by Gerhard Delling in *TDNT* 3.159-60; art. θριαμβεύω by Gerhard Dautzenberg in *EWNT* 2.384-86; art. "Triumphus" by W. Ehlers in PW (1939) 13.493-511; art. "Triumph" by E. Badian in *The Oxford Classical Dictionary* 1095; H. S. Versnel, *Triumphus. An Inquiry into the Origin, Development and Meaning of the Roman Triumph* (Leiden: Brill, 1970); Ernst Künzl, *Der römische Triumph. Siegesfeiern im antiken Rom* (Munich: Beck, 1988); and Michael Mc Cormick, *Eternal Victory. Triumphal rulership in late antiquity, Byzantium and the early medieval West* (Cambridge: Cambridge University Press, 1986) 11-34. I cite here a large number of original sources because Versnel's statement still applies: "many sources which were tapped long ago, have not dried up yet" (*Triumphus* 5). I will comment on the relevance of the so-called "minor triumph," the *ovatio*, in section 9. below, and other specialized studies on 2 Cor 2:14 will also be cited at the appropriate points, primarily, however, in section 11.

[2] Cf. Acts 16:37-39 and 22:25-29, as well as his final imprisonment (and trial) in Rome: chapter 28.

[3] Cf. 1 Cor 9:24-27; Gal 2:2; 5:7; Phil 1:30; 2:16; 3:14; 4:1,3; and 1 Thess 1:19. The combination of athletic and sacrificial imagery in Phil 2:16-17 should be noted in regard to the use of disparate imagery in 2 Cor 2:14-17. On the Isthmian Games, see the art. "Isthmia" by Wolfgang Decker in *Der neue Pauly* (1998) 5.1147-48 and the literature cited there. A survey of Paul's athletic and military imagery, with extensive bibliography, is offered by Edgar Krenz, "Paul, Games, and the Military," in *Paul in the Greco-Roman World*, ed. Paul Sampley (Harrisburg, PA: Trinity Press International, 2003) 344-83, which also applies to section 3. below.

[4] Cf. Tacitus, *The Annals* 2.41 on his conquering Germanic tribes west of the Elbe River.

[5] Cf. Suetonius, "Caligula" 49,2 (in an *ovatio*).

Claudius in 43 CE.⁶ From the founding of Rome until the reign of Vespasian there were more than 320 such triumphs.⁷ Their major importance is shown in Livy 30.15,12, where Scipio says to Masinissa: "there was no higher distinction among the Romans than a triumph...."⁸ In order to grasp the glory⁹ and magnificence of a Roman general's returning from a resounding victory over a declared enemy, and celebrating a triumphal procession through the streets of the capital Rome, viewed by all,¹⁰ one can think of the confetti parade through New York City on June 19, 1945, of the supreme commander of the allied expeditionary forces, General Dwight D. Eisenhower. Returning from victory over the forces of fascism in Europe, he rode through the streets in an open convertible, acclaimed by all,¹¹ similar to a Roman triumphator in his chariot drawn by four white horses in Rome.

Occasioned by an uprising or war waged against Rome by another nation, a triumph, including a triumphal procession,¹² often included the following elements:

---

⁶ Cf. Pliny, *Natural History* 33,54 for his "conquering" Britain. See also the other contemporary examples of *ovatio* cited in section 9. below.

⁷ This figure derives from Paulus Orosius at the beginning of the fifth century CE. Cf. the *Orosii historiarum* 7.9,8 in *Die antike Weltgeschichte in christlicher Sicht*, trans. Adolf Lippolt, 2.158.

⁸ Cf. the statement in Cicero, "In L. Calpurnium Pisonem" 59 (LCL 14.210-11): Julius Caesar in Gaul "burns, he is ablaze with desire for a splendid and a well-earned triumph." See also Plutarch, "Marcus Cato" 11,3, where the consulship and the triumph are the highest honors which can be obtained. I cite at the end of this study the bibliographical information of editions I employ. Most English translations are those of the Loeb Classical Library.

⁹ On the *gloria* of a victorious general, cf. for example Livy, 45.38,8, and 2.47,11, as well as *honor* in 45.39,10 and 3.63,9.

¹⁰ Cf. Josephus, *Bell.* 7,122 on the joint triumph of Vespasian and Titus in 71 CE: "not a soul among that countless host in the city was left at home: all issued forth and occupied every position where it was but possible to stand, leaving only room for the necessary passage of those upon whom they were to gaze." See also Tacitus, *The Annals* 14,13: "all along his [Nero's] route rose tiers of seats of the type used for viewing a triumph."

¹¹ A picture of this occasion is available at the Dwight D. Eisenhower Library in Abilene, Kansas.

¹² Cf. the art. "*Pompa* (πομπή)" by Franz Bömer in PW (1952) 42.1878-1994. In the following I cite primarily examples from Lucius Aemilius Paulus, for the reasons to be explained below. Dio Cassius in his *Roman History*, Book VI from Zonaras 7,21, attempts to describe a typical triumphal procession (LCL 1.192-201). German translations of ten different triumphs are given by Künzl in *Der römische Triumph* 10-13 and 141-50.

1) The appointment by the Senate of a consul (or praetor) as military general, entailing the right of commanding the army in the field (the *imperium*).[13]
2) Before leaving Rome, the general made vows (*vota*) to Iuppiter Optimus Maximus Capitolinus, as the name implies at Jupiter's temple on the Capitol. The vows usually consisted of promising to donate to the god spoils from the military campaign. When the general returned in victory, he then fulfilled these vows.[14]
3) In order for a major triumph to be awarded by the Senate, the general's army had to kill at least 5000 of the enemy's troops.[15]
4) The announcement of the victory in Rome, followed by preliminary ceremonies of thanksgiving (see 2.1 below).
5) Upon the return of the victorious general to Rome, he was not yet allowed to enter the city, but first had to convince the members of the Senate of the legitimacy of their granting him a triumph.[16]
6) Granted the triumph, the general followed with his triumphal procession a prescribed route through Rome, first gathering outside the city limits at the field of Mars (*campus martius*), then entering through the *porta triumphalis*, passing through the racing course of the *circus maximus*, around the Palatine hill, through the *forum*, and finally up to the Capitol hill and the Temple of Jupiter there.[17]
7) In addition to the display on specially constructed wagons of spoils taken on the battlefield and from pillaged enemy settlements, the defeated general was led in chains, often together with his major officers, or a king with his family members. Most often the major

---

[13] Cf. for example Livy 44.17,4 and 10 and Plutarch, "Aemilius Paulus" 10,5 on the consul Lucius Aemilius Paulus for Macedonia, and Livy 44.21,4 and 45.43,2 on Lucius Anicus as a praetor for Illyria.
[14] Cf. Livy 45.39,11.
[15] Cf. Valerius Maximus, "De Iure Triumphi" 2.8,1 in *Memorable Doings and Sayings* (LCL 1.200-01). He wrote in the first third of the first century CE (1.1-3). See also Paulus Orosius, *Orosii historiarum* 5.4,7 (Lippold, *Die antike Weltgeschichte* 2.13).
[16] Cf. Polybius 6.15,8; Dionysius of Halicarnassus, *The Roman Antiquities* 6.30,2-3 and 11.50,1; and the opposition on the part of some to Aemilius Paulus' receiving a triumph in Livy 45.35,4 through 39,20.
[17] Cf. the text and relevant diagrams in Künzl, *Der römische Triumph* 14-19, as well as the art. "Triumph, Triumphzug" by Walter Eder in *Der neue Pauly* (2002) 12/1, 839-41.

opponent was killed just before the end of the procession; sometimes, however, he was allowed to remain alive.[18]

8) In addition to countless others, the general's major officers and his troops walked behind him in the triumphal procession (see 3. below).

9) As in numerous other processions, incense was employed both in the triumphal procession itself, and in the city's temples, especially opened for that occasion (see 2.1.2 below).

10) The final phase of the triumphal procession consisted of sacrifices of thanksgiving at the Capitol, including oxen, wine and incense (see 2.2 below).

Before analyzing those aspects of the triumphal procession which are especially relevant to 2 Cor 2:14-17, I want to suggest why the Apostle Paul thought of and employed triumph imagery at this point.

While Paul mentions "Macedonia" five times elsewhere in his letters,[19] and notes it twice in 1 Cor 16:5, it occurs six times in Second Corinthians. Before 2:14-17 the Apostle refers to it twice in 1:16, "I wanted to visit you on my way to Macedonia, and to come back to you from Macedonia and have you send me on to Judea." This shows Macedonia was a major concern for him already at the beginning of the letter, and it reappears in 2:16. Here Paul says that when he did not find his co-worker Titus in Troas, he said farewell to the Christians there "and went on to Macedonia." The next verse then employs the image of a triumphal procession. Only after the long digression of 3:1 – 7:4 (see the Introduction) does the Apostle pick up the catchword "Macedonia" again in 7:5, "For even when we came into Macedonia...."[20]

On the basis of 2:13; 8:1; 9:2 and 4, most commentators correctly believe that the Jewish Christian Paul wrote Second Corinthians from somewhere in Macedonia. Through a typically Jewish catchword

---

[18] For an example of the first, cf. Josephus, *Bell.* 7.153-54: "The triumphal procession [of Vespasian and Titus] ended at the temple of Jupiter Capitolinus, on reaching which they halted; for it was a time-honoured custom to wait there until the execution of the enemy's general was announced. This was Simon, son of Gioras...." For a special study of the human victims, see the 1951 Tübingen dissertation of Ernst Wallisch, *Die Opfer der römischen Triumphe.* An example of the second is the Macedonian king Perseus in Livy 45.40,6 and 42,4-5.

[19] Rom 15:26; Phil 4:15; 1 Thess 1:7,8 and 4:10.

[20] Cf. the term also in 8:1 and 11:9, as well as "the Macedonians" in 9:2 and 4.

connection,²¹ I suggest that he thought at this point of his namesake, Paulus Macedonicus, and his well-known, magnificent triumphal procession in Rome from November 27-29, 167 BCE²² and therefore employed such imagery in 2:14-17. If correct, this means that there is no break between vv 13 and 14, as so often maintained.

Lucius Aemilius Paul(l)us,²³ born ca. 228 BCE, became a consul and received his first triumph in 182 BCE because of a military victory over the Ligurians.²⁴ In 168 BCE he again became consul at about the age of sixty, was given the *imperium* for the Roman army, consisting of two legions, and defeated the Macedonian King Perseus and his forces at the famous battle of Pydna on June 22 of the same year. Ending within fifteen days a war which had dragged on for four years, Paulus' forces slew more than 25,000 enemy soldiers, with their own losses at only 80 to 100 men.²⁵ Afterwards cutting the Macedonians' taxes in half,²⁶ he

---

²¹ Cf. Strack and Stemberger, *Introduction to the Talmud and Midrash* 21 on the *gezerah shawah*, including the remarks by Saul Lieberman on its being "formed in analogy to the Hellenistic rhetorical term *synkrisis pros ison*."

²² For this exact dating, cf. the *fasti triumphorum* of 167 BCE as illustrated in Künzl, *Der römische Triumph* 59, and 60. See also the art. "Fasti" by G. Schön in PW (1909) 6.2043-45. Even if the reader is more skeptical than I am about this association (Paulos – Paulus), at least sections 1.-3. and 9. below retain their validity.

²³ Cf. the art. "Aemilius Paulus" by E. Klebs in PW (1894) 1.576-80; "L. Ae. Paullus (Macedonicus)" by Hans Georg Gundel in *Der kleine Pauly* (1962) 1.92-93; "Paullus, Lucius Aemilius" in *The Oxford Companion to Classical Literature* 413, which notes that he was "given the cognomen Macedonicus"; "Ae. Paullus, L." by Karl-Ludwig Elvers in *Der neue Pauly* (1996) 1.181-82; and the critical monograph by William Reiter, *Aemilius Paullus. Conqueror of Greece* (London: Croom Helm, 1988). Florus, who probably wrote in the time of Hadrian (117-38 CE), employs the term "Paulus Macedonicus" in his *Epitome of Roman History* 1.31,12. One of Paulus' first two sons, given away for adoption, was the later conqueror of Carthage and then similarly called Scipio "Africanus." See Appian, "The Syrian Wars" 6.

²⁴ Cf. Livy 40.34,7-8 and already 40.25-28.

²⁵ For the latter figure, cf. Plutarch, "Aemilius Paulus" 21,7. See also Livy 44.42,7-8, who in 41,1 says Paulus was now over sixty. For fifteen days, see Appian, *Roman History*, "Macedonian Affairs" 19; for the war's having already lasted four years, see Livy 45.9,2 and 41,5. On the second legion (of two), see Livy 44.41,2 and 42,6. On the battle itself as lasting only one hour, see Plutarch, "Aemilius Paulus" 22,1. The exact date is due to the eclipse of the moon on the night before, June 21. See Livy 44.37,6 and n. 1 in LCL 13.214-15.

²⁶ Cf. Livy 45.18,7.

also granted them their independence.²⁷ After the Macedonian provinces had been reordered, Paulus traveled throughout Greece, including Corinth. There he admired the "world-famous" city's citadel and the isthmus.²⁸ Paulus could thus also later be remembered as having visited Corinth, as Paul the Apostle did. The Macedonian cities were so grateful to Paulus for his generous treatment of them that they sent 400 golden wreaths, each with its own ambassador, to participate as victory prizes in Paulus' triumphal procession.²⁹ The Roman consul, who also knew Greek, was a deeply religious person, having become "one of the priests called Augurs." He "thoroughly understood the religious ceremonial of the ancient Romans" and performed all such duties "with skill and care," later making generous sacrifices to the gods, also in foreign areas.³⁰ Plutarch maintains that Paulus "surpassed his contemporaries" in the virtues of "valour, justice and trustworthiness."³¹ His biographer William Reiter states: "It was to him that Romans of later ages looked in order to discover those attributes which made a man of the Republic."³²

While I shall later call attention to other aspects of Paulus' character which are also relevant to Second Corinthians, at this point the triumphal procession awarded him by the Senate of Rome for his spectacular and speedy victory over King Perseus' numerically superior forces in Macedonia will be analyzed in regard to 2 Cor 2:14-17. Because of the tremendous amount of spoils displayed, it lasted three days. Velleius Paterculus, a Roman army officer, wrote his *Compendium of*

---

[27] Cf. Livy 45.18,1, and Plutarch, "Aemilius Paulus" 28,6.
[28] Cf. Livy 45.28,1-2, and Polybius 30.10,3. This was of course before the destruction of the city by Mummius in 146 BCE and its later establishment as a Roman colony in 46 BCE, when it became the capital of Achaia (see 2 Cor 2:1 - "throughout Achaia").
[29] Plutarch, "Aemilius Paulus" 34,5. Cf. also how the Macedonians who were in Rome at the time of his death not only helped to carry Paulus' bier, but proclaimed him as "benefactor and 'preserver' (σωτήρ)" of their country, his having treated it very kindly after returning to Rome (45.39,8-9).
[30] For the first, cf. Plutarch, "Aemilius Paulus" 3,2-5 and 17,10. On the latter, see for example his sacrifice to Apollo in Delphi, to Jupiter and Hereynus in Lebadia, to Minerva in Athens, and a very large sacrifice in Olympia in Livy 45.27,7 to 28,5. On Paulus' knowledge of Greek, see 45.8,6 and Polybius 29.20,1.
[31] "Aemilius Paulus" 2,6.
[32] Cf. his *Aemilius Paullus* 1. Reiter characterizes the attitudes of Polybius, Livy and Plutarch towards Paulus, each glorifying him in his own style. They downplayed, for example, the sacking and depopulating of Epirus after the Macedonian war (pp. 139-40).

Roman History to appear in 30 CE. He remarks in 1.9,6 regarding Paulus' triumph: "His triumph so far exceeded all former ones, whether in the greatness of King Perses [Perseus of Macedonia] himself, or in the display of statues and the amount of money borne in the procession, that Paulus contributed to the treasury two hundred million sesterces, and by reason of this vast sum eclipsed all previous triumphs by comparison."[33] William Reiter notes that this amount was "so great that the Romans were free from taxes for over one hundred years."[34] Other early writers also comment on the magnificence of Paulus' triumphal procession.[35]

While referred to also by others, an extensive description of this triumphal procession is offered by only three historians. Diodorus of Sicily is known to have been writing his *Library of History* in Greek already in 56 BCE. He describes Paulus' triumphal procession there in 31.8,10-12.[36] Titus Livius (Livy) was born near Padua in 59 BCE and died in 17 CE. In the *Annales*, his history of Rome, he recounts in Latin Paulus' triumph in 45.40,1-6.[37] Plutarch, who lived from the middle of the first century CE to ca. 120 CE, detailed in his *Parallel Lives of Greeks and Romans* the triumphal procession of Paulus in Greek most extensively in his "Aemilius Paulus" 32,2 - 34,8.[38] Accounts of other generals' triumphs supplement the information given in these three narratives in regard to specific aspects.

1. Eternal Triumph

Most generals triumphed only once. Paulus did so twice, once in 182 BCE over the Ligurians, and in 167 BCE over Macedonia. This was true also for Fabius,[39] Marcellus,[40] and Marcus Valerius.[41] Those who

---

[33] On this author, cf. LCL viii.
[34] Cf. his *Aemilius Paullus* 139. See especially Plutarch, "Aemilius Paulus" 38,1.
[35] Cf. Diodorus of Sicily 31.9,1 ("a magnificent triumph") and Dio Cassius from Zonaras in 9,24 ("a most brilliant one").
[36] For the dating, cf. LCL 1.ix; x notes that 36 BCE is the last mentioned date for him.
[37] On these dates, cf. LCL 1.ix; unfortunately, much of the description of the procession has been lost.
[38] On the dating, cf. LCL 1.xi-xii.
[39] Plutarch, "Fabius Maximus" 23,2.
[40] Plutarch, "Marcellus" 22,1.
[41] Plutarch, "Publicola" 20,1-2.

celebrated three triumphs were Romulus[42] and Pompey.[43] The largest number known, however, is four: Furius Camillus[44] and Julius Caesar (d. 44 BCE).[45]

In regard to the latter, Appian notes in *The Civil Wars* 2,106 that it was decreed in Rome "that he should himself sacrifice 'always' (αἰεί) in triumphal costume." After him Augustus (emperor from 31 BCE to 14 CE) created the *ornamenta triumphalia*, granting these to triumphing generals. Yet he relegated the symbolism of victory entirely to himself, solidifying the idea of the emperor as the eternal triumphator. This tendency continued and was even strengthened by his successors.[46]

I would suggest that in stating 2 Cor 2:14, "But thanks be to God, who in Christ 'always' (πάντοτε) leads us in triumphal procession...," Paul not only compares himself favorably with his namesake, Paulus, who only triumphed twice. He also takes a slap here at the ideology or state propaganda regarding the ruling emperor as the "eternal" triumphator. Victory does not "always" belong to the current Roman emperor,[47] who in fact usurps it from his own generals in the battlefield, but to God, who through the Resurrection of His Son Jesus Christ from the dead conquered the powers of sin and death once and for all (1 Cor 15:54-57). Therefore God Himself is in fact the "eternal" triumphator, "always" leading Paul and his co-workers throughout the Mediterranean area, where they attempt to spread the Gospel or fragrance that comes from knowing him (Christ) "in every place." Pompey had triumphed

---

[42] Dionysius of Halicarnassus 2.55,5.
[43] Cicero, "In L. Calpurnium Pisonem" 58; Plutarch, "Comparison of Niceas and Crassus" 2,3; and "Pompey" 45,5, which notes that others before him had celebrated three triumphs, yet he did so over Africa (Libya), Europe and Asia.
[44] Plutarch, "Camillus" 1,1.
[45] Dio Cassius 43.19,1; Appian, *The Civil Wars* 2,101; and Plutarch, "Caesar" 56,7 (cf. 55,2 on three beforehand).
[46] Cf. the evidence gathered in Künzl, *Der römische Triumph*, section "VIII. Ewiger Triumph," pp. 119-33 and 140, as well as Mc Cormick, *Eternal Victory* 11-34 for both Rome and the provinces. The latter notes, for example, that of the ca. thirty new festival days introduced between 45 BCE and 37 CE, "fully one third perpetuate the memory of victories or triumphs" (p. 29), and that there were annual victory games observed also outside the capital (pp. 30-31). On the expression *aeterni triumphi*, see also Valerius Maximus, "De Iure Triumphi" 2.8,5, and "triumph in eternal glory" in 2.8,7.
[47] If this was Nero, who reigned from 54-68 CE, it should be noted that this emperor passed off his musical "successes" in Greece as a triumph, entering Rome in triumphal procession (Suetonius, "Nero" 25). This was a parody of the true meaning of the practice.

over parts of Africa, Europe and Asia, the world as known at that time, and the contemporary emperor attempted to promulgate his victory cult throughout the entire Roman Empire. Yet God commissioned Paul to take the Gospel to "every place," even to Spain, considered the very end of the earth at this time.[48]

2. Thanksgiving, with Incense

When a Roman general was victorious in a major battle, there were usually two thanksgivings. The first occurred when the joyous news first reached Rome, and the second at the end of the general's succeeding triumphal procession.[49]

2.1 Preliminary Thanksgiving

This can be best illustrated by the case of Paulus' victory over King Perseus' army in Macedonia in 168 BCE. First a messenger arrived in Rome and "handed dispatches wreathed in laurel to the consul Gaius Lucinius" (Livy 45.1,6), and the victory over Macedonia was made known (1,9). "Next day the senate met in the senate-house, [and] a 'thanksgiving' (*supplicationes*) was voted..." (2,1). Later the official envoys (*legati*) entered the capital (2,3) and related details of the victory to the Senate. Then at a second meeting shortly thereafter, "Joy (*laetitia*) broke out anew when the consul proclaimed that all sacred buildings should be opened. From the meeting each citizen went of his own accord 'to offer thanks to the gods' (*ad gratias agendas ire dis*), and all over the city the temples of the immortal gods were filled with a huge throng, not only of men, but of women too. The senate, recalled to the senate-house, voted that 'thanksgivings for the glorious achievement (*supplicationes ob rem egregie gestam*)' of the consul Lucius Aemilius

---

[48] Cf. my essay "Paul's Travel Plans to Spain and the 'Full Number of the Gentiles' of Rom. XI 25" in *NovT* 21 (1979) 232-62.

[49] The major study of this topic is by Léon Halkin, *La Supplication d'Action de Graces chez les Romains* (Paris: Les Belles Lettres, 1953). See also the art. "Supplicatio" by Anne Siebert in *Der neue Pauly* (2001) 11.1116. To my knowledge the only person to relate this to 2 Cor 2:14 - although in a very cursory way - is John Fitzgerald, *Cracks in an Earthen Vessel* : An Examination of the Catalogues of Hardships in the Corinthian Correspondence (SBLDS 99; Atlanta: Scholars Press, 1988) 162. However, he thinks that the thanksgiving here was uttered by Paul as a "prisoner of war," making this the "distinctive aspect of the procession" (p. 163). As will be shown below, this is not the case.

[Paulus] should be observed for five days at all the banquet-tables of the gods [the temples], and ordered sacrifice offered with the larger victims" (2,6-8).[50]

A *supplicatio* was "The offering of propitiation to a deity or an instance of it; (esp.) b. (decreed as a thanksgiving after a military victory or sim.)."[51] It generally included prayers, libations and sacrifices.[52] "The principal rite of the thanksgiving ceremony was the *gratulatio*, i.e. the recitation of the official form of prayer by which the Roman people thanked the gods of the victory who came to help the legions." The term *gratulatio* was a synonym for *supplicatio*.[53] Of the sixty-five known cases of a Roman general (*imperator*) receiving a *supplicatio* for his victory, only ten were not connected with a triumph.[54]

This explains why the Apostle Paul, after mentioning Macedonia in 2 Cor 2:13 and having in mind his namesake's tremendous victory there, followed by a five-day period of thanksgiving and later triumph,[55] states just afterwards in v 14: Τῷ δὲ θεῷ χάρις τῷ πάντοτε θριαμβεύοντι ἡμᾶς.... Here χάρις is not grace or favor, but "thanks," "gratitude."[56] Paul at this point does not thank the gods for the Roman legions' military victory on the battlefield, culminating in their general's triumphing in Rome. Instead, he thanks the one God for His victory over sin and death through the Resurrection of His Son Jesus Christ from the dead. It is this God who leads him and his co-workers in a triumphal procession throughout the area of the Mediterranean, where they spread the Gospel. This included Troas, where "a door was opened" to Paul for missionizing (2:12).

---

[50] I slightly modify the translation of Alfred Schlesinger in the LCL. Cf. 2.12 for the dates of the five-day thanksgiving. A three-day thanksgiving had already been decreed in 181 BCE for Paulus' victory over the Ligurians (Livy 40.28,9), and one of unknown length even before this in 189 BCE in regard to his victory over the Lusitanians (37.58,5).
[51] Cf. the *Oxford Latin Dictionary* 1882, which notes numerous examples.
[52] Halkin, *La Supplication* 9.
[53] *Ibid.*, 102. Cf. n. 2, which mentions the expression *grates agere* in the same sense, and *gratulari*.
[54] *Ibid.*, 111.
[55] Contrast the later thanksgiving of fifty days observed at the time of a triumph by Julius Caesar (Dio Cassius, *Roman History* 43.42,2), and the "always" in 2 Cor 2:14.
[56] BAGD 878,5. Cf. also 8:16; 9:15; and especially 1 Cor 15:57, "But thanks be to God, who gives us the victory through our Lord Jesus Christ."

Imagery of Triumph 11

In addition, Paul may be contrasting his giving thanks to God, who leads him in a triumphal procession, to the many days of thanksgiving (*supplicatio*) granted the emperor Nero in 54 CE by the Senate. Here he wore the robe of triumph and entered Rome with the honors of the minor triumph, the *ovatio* (see section 9. below).[57] Finally, it should be noted that the *supplicatio* or thanksgiving for a major military victory included offerings of incense and libations of wine.[58] Since this was also true for the thanksgivings made at the end of the triumphal procession, I include that discussion in the next section.

2.2 Thanksgivings, Including Incense, at the End of the Triumphal Procession

In defending the right of Paulus to celebrate a triumph, Marcus Servilius noted: "No small part of a triumphal procession is formed by 'the sacrificial animals' (*victimae*) going ahead, which makes it clear that the general is returning with 'thanksgiving to the gods' (*dis grates agentem*) for success on behalf of the commonwealth."[59] On the third and last day of Paulus' triumphal procession, "120 stall-fed oxen with gilded horns, bedecked with fillets and garlands," were led along as "victims to the sacrifice" by "young men wearing aprons with handsome borders." Boys in turn attended the latter, "carrying gold and silver vessels of libation (λοιβεῖα)."[60] The λοιβεῖον was a "cup for pouring libations," i.e. drink-offerings,[61] here of wine.

The sacrifice (of thanksgiving) took place before the Temple of Jupiter on the Capitol, the end of the entire triumphal procession. For each ox an offering of incense and wine was made, referred to in the expression *ture ac vino supplicare*.[62] In his description of Scipio's triumphal procession, which Appian considers typical in "The Punic Wars" 66, "a number of incense-bearers" (θυμιατηρίων πλῆθος)[63] came before the general in his chariot. Imagining Tiberius' victory and

---

[57] Cf. Tacitus, *The Annals* 13.8,1, and Halkin, *La Supplication* 120 on this.
[58] Halkin, *La Supplication* 104.
[59] Livy 45.39,12. In 13 he speaks of "all those sacrificial victims."
[60] Plutarch, "Aemilius Paulus" 33,2. On this number of white oxen, cf. Diodorus of Sicily 31.8,12. For them in Scipio's procession, see Appian, "The Punic War" 66.
[61] LSJ 1060, citing this passage and "Marcellus" 2,4: "libation bowls."
[62] Cf. Halkin, *La Supplication* 104, and Siebert, "Supplicatio" 11.1116. For *tus, turis* as incense, see Chambers-Murray 776.
[63] Cf. LSJ 809: censer. The Greek word for incense is θυμίαμα, often in the plural as "fragrant stuffs" for burning (*ibid.*).

triumph over the Germans, Ovid states in *Tristia* 4,2 : "mayhap the lofty Palatium is decked with garlands 'and incense' (*turaque*) is crackling in the fire...." Happy at Julius Caesar's return home, Horace envisions himself comparing it to a triumphal procession: "'O glorious day, with honour to be mentioned!' And as thou takest the lead along the ways, 'Io triumphe!' we will shout all of us together, and not only once: 'Io triumphe!' and 'incense' (*tura*) will we offer to the kindly gods."[64] In his "Aemilius Paulus" 32,3, Plutarch notes that incense was now not only burned as an offering of thanksgiving to Jupiter at the Capitol. "Every temple [in Rome] was open and filled with garlands and 'incense' (θυμιάματα)...." The above references show that at the time of a triumphal procession, the fragrance or aroma of burnt incense was certainly noted by all.

Before each of the 120 oxen in Paulus' triumphal procession was sacrificed, he first presented an offering of incense, burned on a transportable fire pan, onto which wine was poured. This fire pan, next to an ox being killed, is illustrated on a silver goblet from the triumph of Tiberius in 12 CE.[65] Theophrastus, who died ca. 285 BCE, already noted that "the admixture of wine makes some perfumes and 'incenses' (θυμιάματα) more fragrant, for instance myrrh."[66] The expression "more fragrant" (εὐοσμότερα)[67] should be related to the threefold mention of ὀσμή , "fragrance," in 2 Cor 2:14 and 16, also in the context of a triumphal procession (v 14).

After the preliminary offering of incense and wine for each ox, the triumphator spoke a prayer, sprinkled the animal with wine, and passed a sacrificial knife over the animal from head to tail. At this point the

---

[64] Cf. his *The Odes and Epodes* 4.2,46-52 (LCL 290-91).
[65] It is reproduced in Künzl, *Der römische Triumph* 86, middle, where "Opfer vor dem Auszug" should instead read "Opfer zum Abschluss des Zuges."
[66] Cf. his "Odours" 67 in *Enquiry into Plants, and Minor Works on Odours and Weather Signs* (LCL 2.286-87), which I modify. See also 44, to which Georg Wöhrle calls attention in U. Eigler and G. Wöhrle, *Theophrast, De odoribus* 76. See also Ovid, *Metamorphoses* 13,636 on the king of Delos and Aeneas burning incense in the temple of Apollo: "There they burned incense in the flames, poured out wine upon the incense and, according to the customary rite, they slaughtered cattle and burned their entrails in the altar fire...," as well as 7,159-62. For the combination of incense (myrrh) and wine (*potio*, a draught) in the *supplicatio*, see also Festi Fragm. E Cod. Farn. L. XIII (p. 158M) in Sexti Pompei Festi, *De verborum significatu*, ed. Lindsay, pp.150-52. For further details, see Walter Müller, art. "Weihrauch" in PW, Suppl. 15.757-61.
[67] Cf. LSJ 725 on εὐοσμός : sweet-smelling, fragrant.

animal was killed, bled, laid on the side or back, opened, and the entrails cut out and inspected. If approved, the latter, together with other pieces of meat, were placed on the altar for the god (Jupiter) and burned.[68]

In *Bell.* 7.155 Josephus notes that at the conclusion of Vespasian and Titus' triumphal procession at the temple of Jupiter Capitolinus in 71 CE, they "began the sacrifices...duly offered with the customary prayers." The "sacrifices" refer to the animals described above or similar ones. The "customary prayers" (of thanksgiving – *gratulatio*) have in part been reconstructed by Eduard Fraenkel.[69] Basically, they were a reiteration of the vows (*vota*), now fulfilled, the general made in the same temple before going off to the battlefield. At this point he thanked the god(s) for giving his legions victory, for having defeated so many of the enemy, for the great amount of booty, and for preserving the Roman people.[70]

In summary, the typical *supplicatio* or thanksgiving decreed by the Roman Senate at the news of a general's significant victory, coupled with the animal offering of thanksgiving, including incense made more fragrant through the addition of wine, and the prayers of thanksgiving to the god Jupiter on the Capitol at the conclusion of the triumphant procession, appear to have been in the mind of Paul when he thought of his namesake Paulus' victory in Macedonia, from where he wrote Second Corinthians. For this reason, at what is often considered an abrupt change, he can speak in 2:14 of giving thanks to God, who leads him and his fellow workers in the Gospel in a triumphal procession. During this, they spread a very special type of fragrance, also the case in a triumphal procession through the customary use of incense, augmented at the end by wine to make it even more fragrant.

The triumphal procession was a special kind of procession (*pompa* , πομπή). Other processions also contained θυμιατήρια , censers, and participants spreading the fragrance of incense and perfumes. Polybius reports for example that Antiochus IV (Epiphanes) heard of the victory games held by Paulus in Macedonia. Before he opened much more magnificent games at Daphne near Antioch, he had a procession take

---

[68] Cf. the illustration of such a scene from the early second century CE in Künzl, *Der römische Triumph* 80, # 49. I follow his discussion on pp. 82-83 very closely here.

[69] Cf. his *Plautinisches im Plautus* (Berlin: Weidmann, 1922) 234-40, dealing with the speeches of slaves in Plautus who act as if they were a triumphator, and with tablets of triumph set up to commemorate a specific victory.

[70] Scipio's prayer in Livy 29.27,1-5 is typical.

place in 166 BCE with tens of thousands of participants. Among these were "two hundred women sprinkling the crowd with perfumes from golden urns" (30.25,17).[71] Athenaeus also describes Ptolemy Philadelphus' parade in the city stadium of Alexandria ca. 270 BCE, designed to resemble a triumphal procession. In it there were "120 boys in purple tunics, carrying frankincense and myrrh and, moreover, saffron upon gold trenchers." A square altar was carried between two censers (θυμιατήρια), nine feet tall. Before a statue of Dionysius there was "a gold censer on a gold tripod, and two saucers of gold full of cassia and saffron." In the entire procession there were 350 gold censers and gilded altars, and 800 cartloads of spices.[72] Finally, Dionysius of Halicarnassus relates in 7.72,13 that when Aulus Postumius was about to campaign against the Latins and had made his vows, the Roman Senate ordered a festival to be celebrated. It had a parade in which there were dancers, lyre and flute players, "and after them the persons who carried the censers (θυμιατήρια) in which perfumes and frankincense were burned along the whole route of the procession."[73] The use of censers and incense in a special kind of procession, that of the Roman triumph, was thus consistent with the usage in other processions.

One detail of a religious procession in Cenchreae near Corinth may be of relevance to 2 Cor 2:14-17. James Wiseman, a major excavator in Corinth and its environs, reports regarding this harbor town:

> A Sanctuary of Isis was established near the base of the south mole in the 1st century after Christ. At first merely a courtyard with a niche in the southeast end, it was enlarged after the earthquake of A.D. 77 and, by ca. A.D. 100, had grown to include a temple and a large court.[74]

Apuleius, who was probably born ca. 125 CE, describes in his *Metamorphoses*, later designated "The Golden Ass," how a Greek named

---

[71] Cf. Athenaeus, *The Deipnosophists* 5.195b (LCL 2.384-85) on this. W. F. Walbank in *A Critical Commentary on Polybius* (Oxford: Clarendon, 1979) 3.449 notes: "The military aspects of the procession emphasized its resemblance to a Roman triumph...."

[72] Cf. *The Deipnosophists* 5.197f, 198b-d, 201e, 202b and f, as well as the frankincense and myrrh of 201a.

[73] For other examples of incense in a procession, cf. Bömer, art. "*Pompa* (πομπή)" in PW 42. 1918, 1923, 1932, 1937 and 1964.

[74] Cf. his art. "Corinth and Rome I: 228 B.C. - A.D. 267" in *Aufstieg und Niedergang der römischen Welt*, II. 7/1, 438-548, here p. 531. See also Bömer, art. "*Pompa* (πομπή)" in PW 42.1947 on this.

Lucius was transformed into an ass. Arriving at the town of Cenchreae, he falls asleep on the shore, where Queen Isis reveals her name to him in a dream. Suddenly people in a "triumphant mood" mill about in all the streets, the "great procession" (*pompae magnae*) of the savior goddess now beginning. Some in it "shook out drops of delightful balsam and other ointments to sprinkle the streets." When Lucius eats a wreath of roses held out to him by a priest, he becomes human again. Then the priests of Isis tell him: "Join the procession of the savior goddess with triumphant step!" In doing so, he "triumphs over his Fortune." When the procession reaches the seashore, the high priest consecrates a model ship, which is filled with spices and other offerings and set into the waters. Then its bearers return to the shrine of Isis, where a priest declares the opening of the navigation season in Greek: τὰ πλοιαφεσία (ship launching).[75]

Apuleius, who wrote both in Greek and Latin, here describes the Isis procession with balsam and other ointments being sprinkled on the streets, causing fragrant aromas, as he may well have himself encountered it there in the second century CE. It should be noted that he employs imagery of the "triumph" three times in his description, showing how fluid such language was. The cult of Isis probably existed in Cenchreae before 77 CE, although on a much smaller scale.[76] If it already had a major ship-launching procession of Isis before this, which makes good sense for a harbor town which hosted many ships until the beginning of the spring sailing season, not only Phoebe with her house church in Cenchreae (Rom 16:1)[77] would have been well aware of the fragrant aromas of balsam and other ointments, sprinkled during the

---

[75] Cf. Apuleius' *Metamorphoses* 10-11. For the dating, see 1.ix. On τὰ πλοιαφεσία as the "*launching of the ship* of Isis, a festival," see LSJ 1422 with other references. Pausanius, who was still writing his *Description of Greece* ca. 175 CE (LCL 1.ix), mentions in 2.2,3 that at one end of the harbor of Cenchreae there were then "sanctuaries of Asclepius and of Isis."

[76] Cf. Robert Scranton, Joseph Shaw and Leila Ibrahim, *Kenchreai, Eastern Port of Corinth*, I: Topography and Architecture (Leiden: Brill, 1978) 53-78, esp. 72-4 by Robert Scranton, and illustrations XXII-XXIII B on the sanctuary of Isis there. The Egyptian cult of Isis had already reached Athens ca. 330 BCE, and Rome ca. 200 BCE. See Hans-Josef Klauck, *The Religious Context of Early Christianity*. A Guide to Graeco-Roman Religions (Edinburgh: Clark, 2000) 132-33.

[77] Cf. Acts 18:18, which states that Paul, under a (Nazirite) vow, had his hair cut at Cenchreae. The fact that he could easily have had this done already in Corinth shows that someone from the house church in the harbor town most probably did this for him.

procession. The inhabitants of Corinth, only some 9 km (5.4 m) away, where Paul stayed and missionized for a year and a half according to Acts 18:11, would certainly also have been familiar with it and may even have thought of it when they heard 2 Cor 2:14-17, with its imagery of fragrance and aroma and a triumphal procession, read at their church assembly / assemblies. More, unfortunately, cannot be said.

3. *The Triumphator and His Officers in the Triumphal Procession*

In 2 Cor 2:14 Paul writes: "But thanks be to God, who in Christ always leads us in triumphal procession...." God is obviously not a Roman general, celebrating a previous military victory on the battlefield by a triumphal procession through the streets of Rome. The Apostle thus employs the term θριαμβεύω in a *metaphorical* sense. The occurrence of a related term in the OT helped him to do so.

In Rom 9:29 Paul quotes LXX Isa 1:9 : " If 'the Lord of hosts' had not left survivors to us...." The term Κύριος Σαβαώθ here in the LXX is based on the MT's יהוה צְבָאוֹת.[78] A צָבָא is an "army,"[79] also designated a "host." The usual expression in the MT is the longer "the Lord God of hosts."[80]

In early Judaism the angels were considered to be the warriors of the Lord, making up His army / host. An example is *Gen. Rab.* Vayyishlach 75/10 on Gen 32:4 (Eng. 3), "And Jacob sent messengers / angels before him." Since v 3 (Eng. 2) mentions God's camp, the midrash asks a question and answers it itself: "Of how many did the camp of God consist? Two thousand myriads of ministering angels," which is based on Ps 68:18. To explain the term "two camps" (Mahanaim) in v 3 (Eng. 2), the midrash says this teaches "that four thousand ministering angels disguised themselves for Jacob's sake, and they all looked like king's troops; some were clad in armour, others were horsemen, others again were charioteers."[81] An example from the Gospels is found in Luke 2:13. Suddenly there was with the angel who had just announced to shepherds near Bethlehem that a Savior, the Messiah, was born that day:

---

[78] Cf. the concordance of Hatch-Redpath 1256.
[79] BDB 838.
[80] BDB 839,4. See also the art. צְבָאוֹת by H.-J. Zobel in *TWAT* (1989) 6.876-92. A popular etymology is found in 1 Sam 17:45 – "the Lord of hosts, the God of the armies of Israel."
[81] Theodor and Albeck 888-89, Soncino 2.695-96. Other examples are found in 78/11 on Gen 33:8 (Theodor and Albeck 929, Soncino 2.722), and in *Midr. Pss.* 5/7 on the legions of angels who precede God (Buber 54, Braude 1.87-88).

"a multitude of 'the heavenly host' (στρατιᾶς οὐρανίου)," which then proceeds to praise God. They are angels, who then return to heaven (v 15).

In Judaic and NT sources God can thus be pictured as the general or commander of His heavenly army / host, consisting of the angels.

At another point in Second Corinthians Paul also employs martial imagery. In 10:3-4 he characterizes himself and his co-workers as a special kind of "soldiers" in spreading the Gospel: "'we do' not 'wage war' (στρατευόμεθα)[82] according to human standards, for the weapons of our 'warfare' (στρατιᾶς)[83] are not merely human, but they have power to destroy strongholds." Other passages such as 6:7, "with the weapons of righteousness for the right hand and for the left," Phil 2:25 on Epaphroditus as "my brother and co-worker and fellow soldier," Plmn 2 on "Archippus our fellow soldier" (both are συστρατιώτης), and 1 Thess 5:8 on "the breastplate of faith and love" and "for a helmet the hope of salvation" show that Paul in 2 Cor 2:14 can describe himself and his co-workers[84] metaphorically as soldiers participating in their general's, the Lord God of hosts', triumphal procession. They are not to be imagined as the captured enemy general and his major officers. At least the first was most often grimly executed at the end of the triumphal procession.[85] Rather, they are thought of as the triumphing general's main officers, who walked right behind him or rode next to him[86] in the procession, followed by the regular soldiers. Various passages attest this, but first a note about the organization of a Roman army is helpful.

A consular army usually had two legions,[87] which was also true for Paul's namesake Paulus in Macedonia.[88] The consul received the

---

[82] Cf. BAGD 770 on στρατεύω , middle.
[83] Cf. BAGD 770 on στρατιά , "army." For a special study of these verses' military imagery in relationship to similar imagery in the philosophers, see Abraham Malherbe, "Antisthenes and Odysseus, and Paul at War," in *HTR* 76 (1983) 143-73, esp. 166, n. 131.
[84] This imagery also argues for taking the "we" and "us" forms, at least at this point, as meant literally and not as the authorial plural.
[85] Cf. Josephus, *Bell.* 7.153, and Appian, "The Mithridatic Wars" 117 with Aristobulus, king of the Jews.
[86] For two examples of this, cf. Appian, "The Mithridatic Wars" 117, and Cicero, "L.Calpurnium Pisonem" 60.
[87] Cf. Graham Webster, *The Roman Imperial Army of the First and Second Centuries A.D.* (London: Black, 1985³) 19, n. 2. His first chapter is a history of the army before that time. See also Michael Grant, *The Army of the Caesars* (London: Weidenfeld and Nicolson, 1975).
[88] See Livy 45.35,8 for a reference to the second legion in Macedonia.

imperium or official command, thus becoming the *imperator* or general. Each legion was headed by a *legatus*, under whom were six military *tribuni*. For each of the legion's ten cohorts there were six *centuriones*, subject to the tribunes.[89] In addition, the legion had cavalrymen.[90]

Livy notes in 31.49,10 regarding the Romans: "Their ancestors had ordained that the legates, tribunes, centurions and even the common soldiers should attend a triumph, to the end that the Roman people might see the witnesses to the deeds of the man to whom so signal an honor was given."[91] Indeed, when soldiers were lacking in the triumphal procession, it was noted as unusual.[92] The centurion Tullius in his remarks to the triumphator Sulpicius expresses, for example, the soldiers' feeling of "triumphing with" their general. Livy notes in 7.13,10 that Tullius says: "We are eager not only to conquer, but to conquer under your leadership; to win for you the glorious laurel; to enter the City with you in the march of triumph (*tecum triumphantes*); and following your chariot, to approach the throne of Jupiter Optimus Maximus, expressing thanks and rejoicing (*gratantes ovantesque adire*)."

Appian in *The Civil Wars* 2,93 also has Julius Caesar tell his mutinous soldiers: "And I shall give you all that I have promised 'when I triumph with other soldiers' (ὅταν θριαμβεύσω μεθ᾽ ἑτέρων)." The troops then considered that "others would join in the triumph instead of themselves (θριαμβεύσουσι δ᾽ ἀνθ᾽ αὐτῶν ἕτεροι), and they would lose the gains of the war in Africa." Here it is also clearly expressed that the (officers and) soldiers share directly in the victorious general's triumph and procession.[93]

When Augustus and Tiberius celebrated a triumph, not only Germanicus but also the other commanders received the *ornamenta triumphalia*.[94] Tiberius returned to Rome from Germany in 12 CE and also celebrated a triumph. He was "accompanied by his generals, for

---

[89] Cf. Webster, *The Roman Imperial Army* 109-15, and Grant, *The Army* xxxii - xxxiii.
[90] Cf. for example Pliny, *Natural History* 15,19; Dionysius of Halicarnassus 2.34,2; and Livy 36.40,13.
[91] I slightly alter the translation of Evan Sage in the LCL.
[92] Cf. Livy 31.49,3 and especially 37.46,6.
[93] I owe this reference to Cilliers Breytenbach, "Paul's Proclamation and God's 'Thriambos.' Notes on 2 Corinthians 2:14-16b" in *Neotestamentica* 24 (1990) 260. For an emphasis on Paulus' triumph as also the soldiers' triumph, cf. Livy 45.38,14 ("celebrating your triumph"). See also 38,3.
[94] Cf. Dio Cassius 56.17,1-2.

whom he had obtained the *triumphalia ornamenta*."[95] Desiring a "legitimate triumph," Claudius took a part of Britain "without any battle or bloodshed," returned to Rome and "celebrated a triumph of great splendor" in 44 CE. "Those who had won the triumphal regalia in the same war," certainly his major officers, rode in a carriage behind him.[96]

Some officers repeatedly participated in triumphal processions. Aulus Gellius, writing in regard to the tribune Lucius Sicinius Dentatus, notes for example in 2.11,4 that "he took part with his generals in nine triumphal processions."[97] Often decorations and money were distributed to the soldiers just before they entered Rome for their general's triumphal procession. Livy notes regarding the triumph of Gnaeus Manlius in 39.7,2 for example that "men of all ranks, presented with military decorations, followed his car."

Often the soldiers sang rude verses during the procession, at times making fun of their general or a subordinate officer. Yet numerous cases are also known of their praising the main commander. Livy notes for example in 45.38,12 : "Soldiers indeed are directly interested in the matter [of the triumph], for they too are crowned with laurel, while each man is adorned with the decorations he has been given; they parade through the city [of Rome] invoking the spirit of Triumphus by name and singing their own praises and those of their general."[98] This was also true for Paulus' triumph. Plutarch in "Aemilius Paulus" 34,7 notes that "The whole army also carried sprays of laurel, following the chariot of their general by companies and divisions, and singing, some of them divers songs intermingled with jesting, as the ancient custom was, and other paeans of victory and hymns in praise of the achievements of Aemilius...."[99]

All of the above, especially the officers' marching behind or riding beside the chariot of the triumphator general, with the regular soldiers' singing his praises, rejoicing with him, and triumphing with him because of the major victory he has achieved, cause me to interpret 2 Cor 2:14 in a positive way. God, the Lord of hosts / armies, also leads Paul

---

[95] Cf. Suetonius, "Tiberius" 20.
[96] Cf. Suetonius, "Claudius" 17. Dio Cassius 60.23,2 thinks the latter were senators, but Suetonius is to be preferred.
[97] Cf. already Valerius Maximus, "De Iure Triumphi" 3.2,24 on him, as well as Dionysius of Halicarnassus 10.36,2, and Pliny, *Natural History* 7,102.
[98] Cf. also 10.30,9 and 45.43,8.
[99] Cf. also Plutarch, "Marcellus" 8,2 for the army's "singing odes composed for the occasion, together with paeans of victory in praise of the god [Jupiter] and their general," as well as Dionysius of Halicarnassus 2.34,2.

and his co-workers in a triumphal procession throughout the Mediterranean area, where they spread the Gospel, the good news of God's victory over sin and death through the Resurrection of His Son, Jesus Christ, from the dead. Like the Roman triumphator general, God leads them as His major officers in a triumphal procession, not through the city of Rome, but throughout the entire Mediterranean area. Jean Calvin notes in this regard that the common meaning of θριαμβεύω, that of prisoners being led in triumph, is not meant in 2 Cor 2:14. Rather,

> Paul means that he had a share in the triumph that God was celebrating because it was through his work that it was won, just as the chief lieutenants shared the general's triumph by riding on horseback beside his chariot. Thus since all ministers of the Gospel fight under God's banner and win for Him the victory and the honour of a triumph, He honours each of them with a share in His triumph according to his rank in the army and the efforts he has made. Thus they hold a triumph, but it is not their own, but God's.[100]

Calvin is followed in his interpretation by numerous other commentators.[101]

The image of θριαμβεύω in 2 Cor 2:14 is clearly metaphorical, employed by the Apostle Paul in a relatively infrequent way,[102]

---

[100] Cf. *The Second Epistle of Paul the Apostle to the Corinthians*, trans. T. Smail (Calvin's Commentaries; Grand Rapids, Michigan: Eerdmans, 1996) 33-34.

[101] Cf. Hans Windisch, *Der zweite Korintherbrief* (Meyer; Göttingen: Vandenhoeck & Ruprecht, 1924⁹) 97, who views Paul as actively participating in a positive way in the triumphal procession, perhaps as an officer or soldier; Werner Kümmel in his additions to Hans Lietzmann, *An die Korinther I-II* (HNT 9; Tübingen: Mohr Siebeck, 1949⁴) 198; Heinz-Dietrich Wendland, *Die Briefe an die Korinther* (NTD 7; Göttingen: Vandenhoeck & Ruprecht, 1964¹⁰) 152; Jean Héring, *The Second Epistle of Saint Paul to the Corinthians* (London: The Epworth Press, 1967) 18 ("like a victorious general"); C. K. Barrett, *The Second Epistle to the Corinthians* (Black's; London: Adam and Charles Black, 1973²) 98; and F. F. Bruce, *1 and 2 Corinthians* (NCB; London: Oliphants, 1978) 187. See already Augustine here on Paul as "this most intrepid soldier" ("Predestination of the Saints" 20,41 in *Ancient Christian Commentary on Scripture*, New Testament VII, 1-2 Corinthians, 209).

[102] This is why the famous lexicographers Henry Liddell, Robert Scott and Henry Jones (LSJ) can only cite 2 Cor 2:14 for this meaning of θριαμβεύω (806,2): "*lead in triumph*, as a general does his army, metaph., ἡμᾶς ἐν Χριστῷ." Paul's use had of necessity to be metaphorical, for "it was forbidden a private individual to

positively. It does not allude here to a captured enemy general led in chains before the chariot of the triumphator, to be grimly executed at the end of the procession. Instead, the entire mood is positive, full of joy in thanksgiving (χαρά).

While up to now only Paul and very few others are known to have employed θριαμβεύω , *triumpho* and *ovo* (see 9. below) in exactly this way, other writers also used the verb (and its Latin equivalent, together with their cognate nouns) metaphorically, showing that the Apostle was neither the first nor the last to do so.

Cicero, who died in 43 BCE, was once asked when away from Rome whether there was any hope of a "triumph" (*triumphi*). He replied: "I would have quite a glorious triumph (*triumpharem*) if only in the shortening of the period of my yearning for all that is dearest to me."[103] Cicero also relates that when Catilene thought he was victorious over members of the Senate, he raced from there "joyously triumphant" (*triumphans gaudio*).[104] The famous orator also remarks regarding a certain Sassia in court: "then does this exemplary, this illustrious mother make display of her delight, revelling and rejoicing in her triumph (*triumphare gaudio coepit*) not over her lust but over her daughter."[105] The last two examples, connecting "to triumph" with "delight," corroborate my *positive* interpretation of θριαμβεύω in 2 Cor 2:14, connected with thanksgiving.

Ovid, who died in 18 CE, in "The Amores" 2,12 pictures himself as the lover of a girl named Corinna. He describes himself in terms of a victorious general celebrating his (bloodless) triumph (*triumphus*). Indeed, Ovid was the entire army. In 1,2 he notes that Cupid is a triumphator, and he himself one of his recent spoils. Ovid remarks concerning those couples whom Cupid has caused to fall in love with each other that this procession will be a magnificent triumph (*triumphus*) for him. Conscience, modesty, and all those opposed to the "camp of Love" will be led along as captives with their hands tied

---

hold a triumph" (Dio Cassius, *Roman History* 6 from Zonaras 7,21 [LCL 1.192-93]).
[103] Cf. the "Epistulae ad Familiares" 2.12,3.
[104] Cf. "Pro Murena" 25,51.
[105] Cf. "Pro Cluentio" 5,14. I owe these references and in part the translations to Peter Marshall, "A Metaphor of Social Shame: θριαμβεύειν in 2 Cor. 2:14," in *NovT* 25 (1983) 305.

behind their backs, the crowd shouting: "*Io Triumphe!*" He also remarks: "I am yours to be part of your 'sacred triumph' (*sacri...triumphi*)."[106]

Valerius Maximus, who was active until at least 31 CE,[107] wrote in "De Iure Triumphi" 2.8,5: "Scipio and Marcellus, whose very names are like an everlasting triumph (*aeterni triumphi*)...." In 2.8,7 he also makes a comparison with triumph imagery: "With [an oak wreath granted Augustus by the Senate in 27 BCE] the doorposts of the Augustus dwelling 'triumph in eternal glory' (*sempiterna gloria triumphant*)."

Seneca, who died in 65 CE, also writes metaphorically in "De Vita Beata" 25,4 about a philosopher like Socrates: "Make me victor over the nations of the world, let the voluptuous car of Bacchus convey me 'in triumph' (*triumphantem*) from the rising of the sun all the way to Thebes...." Other allusions here to the triumphal procession of a Roman general are the term *fericulum*, a "structure on which the spoils and sometimes noble captives were displayed in the triumphal procession,"[108] and the sentence: "the procession (*pompam*) of a proud and brutal victor; no whit more humble shall I be when I am driven [as a captive] in front of the chariot of another than when I stood erect upon my own."[109]

Epictetus, who died ca. 120 CE, like the Apostle Paul also employed the verb θριαμβεύω in a comparison. In 3.24,85 he makes the following recommendation: "if you kiss your child, your brother, your friend, never allow your fancy free rein, nor your exuberant spirits to go as far as they like, but hold them back, stop them, *just like* those who stand behind generals 'when they ride in triumph' (τοῖς θριαμβεύουσιν), and keep reminding them that they are mortal. In such fashion do you too remind yourself that the object of your love is mortal...."[110]

---

[106] Ovid also emphasizes the motif of joy here in regard to Cupid: "All joyously as thou dost pass in triumph..." (1,39). Cf. also his *Metamorphoses* 1 (LCL 1.40-41) regarding the "shouts of joy" which shall acclaim the triumph of Roman generals.

[107] Cf. the *Memorable Doings and Sayings*, LCL 1.1-3.

[108] Cf. n. "d" by John Basore in the LCL edition of *Seneca. Moral Essays* 2.167. See also n. "c" in 2.166-67 on Bacchus as "here pictured as returning from his triumphal journey to India."

[109] See also Seneca's "De Beneficiis" 2.11,1 for another comparison with a triumph. On another instance of a πομπή as probably a triumphal procession, cf. the comparison made by Josephus in *Ant.* 14,45 - "as if they were marching in a festive procession instead of pleading their cause."

[110] On the apotropaic purpose of such behavior by a slave, cf. n. 1 in LCL 2.212-13, and Juvenal, *Satires* 10,41-42. I owe this reference to Cilliers Breytenbach,

The above examples from Cicero, Ovid, Valerius Maximus, Seneca and Epictetus clearly demonstrate that the terms "triumph" and "to triumph" (*triumphus, triumphare*, θρίαμβος, θριαμβεύειν) were also used metaphorically in new ways by writers both before and after the Apostle Paul. This shows that he too could employ θριαμβεύω in a relatively infrequent, metaphorical manner: God, the Lord of hosts, "leads in a triumphal procession" Paul and his co-workers, as a Roman general leads his officers and soldiers behind his victory chariot in his triumphal procession through the city of Rome. Yet their realm for triumphing with God in His victory over sin and death through the Resurrection of His Son, Jesus Christ, from the dead is not confined to one locality. It is "in every place," throughout the Mediterranean area.

* * *

Other motifs from the Apostle Paul's namesake, the Roman general Paulus and his victory over Macedonia and its King Perseus (sections 4.-8.), and from the imagery of the triumph in general (sections 9.-10.), are also of relevance to Second Corinthians.

4. Centers for the Collection of Money, and the Offerings of First-fruits in the Jerusalem Temple

After his decisive victory over King Perseus of Macedonia at Pydna in 168 BCE, Paulus divided the country into four regions or cantons for administrative purposes, each with its capital city: 1) Amphipolis; 2) Thessalonica; 3) Pella; and 4) Pelagonia. Diodorus of Sicily in 31.8,9 notes that governors (ἀρχηγοί) were established, "and here the taxes were collected (καὶ οἱ φόροι ἠθροίζοντο)." In 45.29,9 Livy relates this in his own words: "In those places Paulus ordered an assembly of each region to be appointed, 'money to be gathered (*pecuniam conferri*),' and magistrates elected."[111] While Plutarch in "Aemilius Paulus" 28,6 does not give the above details, he notes the following: "When the ten

---

"Paul's Proclamation" 264. See also Plutarch, "Antony" 84,4, where Cleopatra holds the urn with Antony's ashes and asks him not to "permit a triumph to be celebrated over thyself in my person...."

[111] In Pompeius Trogus' world history 33,2, he also notes that officials were appointed by Paulus in the individual communities. Cf. M. *IVNIANI IVSTINI, EPITOMA HISTORIARUM PHILIPPICARUM POMPEI TROGI*, ed. Otto Seel, 240, and his German translation in Pompeius Trogus, *Weltgeschichte von den Anfängen bis Augustus, im Auszug des Justin* 391.

commissioners arrived from Rome, he [Paulus] restored to the Macedonians their country and their cities for free and independent residence; they were also to pay the Romans a hundred talents in tribute, a sum less than half of what they used to pay their kings." As remarked above, the Macedonians were so grateful for this gesture on the part of Paulus that representatives of 400 of their cities voluntarily marched with golden wreaths in his triumphal procession the next year in Rome, and those resident there at the time of his death, out of gratitude for his positive treatment of them, participated in his funeral procession.

I suggest that the Apostle Paul was inspired in part by his namesake Paulus when he set up centers for the collection of money he wished to take along to Jerusalem in order to "remember the poor" (Christians) there (Gal 2:10; cf. 2 Cor 9:12). In Romans 15 the Apostle relates that he is now going to Jerusalem "in a ministry to the saints" (v 25), "for Macedonia and Achaia have been pleased to share their resources with the poor among the saints at Jerusalem" (v 26). When Paul has completed this and has "sealed to them this 'fruit' (καρπός)," he will set out by way of Rome to Spain (v 28). In 1:13 the Apostle expresses his hope that "I may reap some 'fruit' (καρπός) among you as I have among the rest of the Gentiles." This "fruit" most probably in part also refers to a monetary contribution to Paul's collection enterprise.[112]

Macedonia certainly included as collection points for the Apostle Philippi; Thessalonica, the capital of the Roman province of Macedonia; and Beroea (cf. Acts 20:4). Corinth, which Paulus had visited after conquering Macedonia, was now the capital of the Roman province of Achaia (2 Cor 1:1), which included all of southern Greece. In Second Corinthians Paul devotes two whole chapters to this collection enterprise (8-9), which has been estimated to have taken Paul eight years up to the time of the writing of Romans, showing how important it was to him.[113]

Paul not only can designate his collection of money for the poor Christians in Jerusalem / Judea "fruit";[114] he also designates new

---

[112] For harvest imagery in connection with the collection, cf. 2 Cor 9:6-10.
[113] Cf. Keith Nickle, *The Collection. A Study in the Strategy of Paul* (London, 1966) 92, n. 137. He should also be consulted for the relevance of the Jewish sheqel Temple tax and its collection in the Diaspora to Paul's collection enterprise.
[114] Elsewhere, for example in 1Cor 16:3 and 2 Cor 8:4, 6-7, 19 he labels it "grace" (χάρις), "a generous undertaking."

Imagery of Triumph

converts as "first-fruits," ἀπαρχή,[115] in Rom 16:5, 1 Cor 16:15 (Stephanus in Achaia), and 2 Thess 2:13. Representatives or delegates of the congregations founded by him, who as new Christians could also be thought of as "first-fruits," accompanied the Apostle of the Gentiles to Jerusalem.[116] On what turned out to be his last journey to the city, Paul "eagerly" wanted to be there by Pentecost (Acts 20:16). This was certainly in part because the festival of Pentecost was held at the conclusion of the Feast of Weeks,[117] when the first-fruits (ἀπαρχή) were offered in the Jerusalem Temple. Texts such as Deut 26:1-11, Lev 23:9-21 and Num 28:26-31 describe it and its offerings and lie behind the Mishnah tractate "Bikkurim" ("First-fruits").

A *ma ʿamad* (מַעֲמָד) was "a group of representatives from outlying districts, corresponding to the twenty-four 'courses of priests.' Part of them went up to the Temple as witnesses of the offering of the sacrifices..., and part came together in their own town, where they held prayers at fixed times during the day coinciding with the fixed times of sacrifice in the Temple."[118] Representatives of the smaller towns gathered in the town of the *ma ʿamad* and proceeded from there to Jerusalem (*m. Bikk.* 3:2). Before this entourage went an ox, to be used as a peace-offering, with "horns overlaid with gold and a wreath of olive-leaves on its head" (3:3), reminiscent of the oxen led before the Roman general in his triumphal procession, to become a thanksgiving offering before and in the Temple of Jupiter. "Flute-players[119] went before them until they reached the Temple Mount" (3:4), also reminiscent of the flutes played in the *ovatio* form of the triumphal procession (see section 9. below). When the *ma ʿamad* reached the Temple Court, the Levites sang Ps 30:2-13 (Eng. 1-12), the first-fruits were taken from the men's

---

[115] BAGD 81,b.
[116] Cf. 1 Cor 16:3 (v 4 shows that this was before Paul definitely decided to go himself to Jerusalem); 2 Cor 8:19, 23; 9:3; and Acts 20:4.
[117] Cf. the art. "Weeks, Feast of" by J. Rylaarsdam in *IDB* 4.827-28. It is also known as the "Feast of Harvest," "Pentecost" and "Day of First Fruits" (see the references on p. 827).
[118] Cf. Danby, *The Mishnah* 794, and Jastrow 818,3), as well as *m. Ta ʿan.* 4:2 (Danby 199). See also *t. Bikk.* 2:8 (Zuckermandel / Liebermann 101, Neusner 2.349), which also includes a description of the various kinds of fruits, and *y. Bikk.* 3:2, 65c (Neusner 10.195) on which psalms were sung when by the *ma ʿamar*.
[119] Cf. Jastrow 468 on חָלִיל as a flute, and הֶחָלִיל here as the flute-players. See also *m. ʿArak.* 2:3 (Albeck 5.200, Danby 545).

baskets and offered by the priests, and the entourage returned home after spending the night in Jerusalem.[120]

The ox described above as a peace-offering (*m. Bikk.* 2:4; 3:3) was included in the offerings prescribed for the Festival of Weeks in Num 28:26-31 as a burnt offering, "a fragrant odor" to the Lord (v 27). The latter expression is רֵיחַ נִיחֹחַ,[121] in the LXX ὀσμὴ εὐωδίας . It should also be noted that the first-fruits of the harvest were one of the grain offerings, described in Lev 2:1-16. "Frankincense" (לְבֹנָה , LXX λίβανος) was added to the offering of first-fruits (vv 1 and 15-16), making it aromatic. When such a grain offering was burnt upon the altar, it also produced a "pleasing odor" to the Lord (vv 9 and 12, with the Hebrew and Greek as above). The two terms within the expression ὀσμὴ εὐωδίας employed here in the offerings made at the Festival of Weeks, also called Pentecost, are precisely those used by the Apostle Paul in 2 Cor 2:14-16.

It is hard to imagine that the converted Jew Paul did not think of the gilded ox, flute players and sacrifices in the Jerusalem Temple, including frankincense, producing a "fragrant odor" to the Lord, when he too accompanied representatives of the congregations he had founded with their monetary "fruit" for the poor saints in Jerusalem at Pentecost. Some of his "first-fruits" may have traveled with him, forming an entourage like that of the *ma 'amar*. The above imagery, certainly known to the Jewish Christian Paul from personal observance of the Feast of Weeks / Pentecost,[122] may also have reminded him of similar phenomena in a triumphal procession, another possible reason for his employing ὀσμή and εὐωδία in 2 Cor 2:14-16.[123]

5. *Suspicion of Fiscal Impropriety*

At two points in Second Corinthians the Apostle Paul defends himself against the allegation that, although ostensibly earning his own living and taking no monetary remuneration from the Corinthians while

---

[120] On *m. Bikk.* 3:1-6, cf. Albeck 1.318-20 and Danby 96-97, and 2:4 on spending the night in Jerusalem.

[121] Cf. BDB 926 on רֵיחַ as odor, and 629 on נִיחֹחַ , the phrase always translated in the LXX as ὀσμὴ εὐωδίας.

[122] This would be especially true if Paul had studied in Jerusalem at the feet of Gamaliel (Acts 22:3) and had a sister, or at least a nephew, there (23:16).

[123] Cf. also Dionysius of Halicarnassus 2.35,1, where Romulus in a triumph is described as offering to the gods "the sacrifices of thanksgiving and 'the first-fruits' (ἀπαρχάς) of victory...," that is, the best part of the spoils taken in war. See also 34,1.

missionizing there,[124] he secretly would appropriate to himself part of the money collected from them for the poor Christians in Jerusalem / Judea.[125]

In 7:2 Paul states: "we have wronged no one, we have corrupted no one, 'we have taken advantage' of no one." The latter Greek verb is πλεονεκτέω, to "take advantage of, outwit, defraud, cheat" someone.[126] This verb reoccurs twice in 12:16-18. In v 14 the Apostle notes that when he comes to the Corinthians a third time, he will not burden them "because I do not want what is yours but you." Then he continues this argumentation in vv 16-18: "Let it be assumed that I did not [on previous stays in Corinth] burden you. Nevertheless you say since I was crafty, I took you in by deceit. 17) Did I 'take advantage of' you through any of those I sent to you? 18) I urged Titus to go, and sent the brother with him. Titus did not 'take advantage of' you, did he? Did we not conduct ourselves with the same spirit? Did we not take the same steps?"

Here Paul feels forced to employ quite strong language in defending his own fiscal propriety because others in Corinth – some of his opponents there – maintain he is craftily exploiting them through his collection enterprise. His self-defense recalls what happened to his namesake, Paulus, in connection with his triumph, and the Apostle may have that episode in mind here, knowing that his own character is just as unimpeachable as was that of Paulus.

When Paulus was about to celebrate his triumph in Rome, "defamation" (*obstrectatio*) attacked him according to Livy in 45.35,5.[127] Servius Sulpicius Galba, military tribune of the second legion in Macedonia, "was personally hostile to the general" (35,8) and attempted to prevent Paulus from triumphing by having his soldiers vote this down for such a domineering and "stingy" leader, who "was unable to give them money" (35,9).[128] The latter refers to the soldiers' opinion that

---

[124] Elsewhere he argues that he has the right to do so: 1 Cor 9:4.
[125] Alfred Plummer in *The Second Epistle of St Paul to the Corinthians* (Edinburgh: Clark, 1915 / 1960) 364 on v 16 aptly remarks regarding this allegation: "he and his friends collected money for the poor saints, and some of it stuck to his fingers." Cf. also C. K. Barrett, *The Second Epistle to the Corinthians* 324: Paul is thought to have "pocketed the proceeds himself." Barrett's arguments for chapters 10-13 having been written after 8-9 are very plausible.
[126] BAGD 667,1. The second verb, φθείρω, may also mean to ruin someone financially (BAGD 857,1.a.), but this is not certain.
[127] Cf. 39,16 on his speech as "of a slanderous and malicious sort."
[128] In 45.37,1 Livy characterizes him as "a personal enemy of such high rank, so rash, and so eloquent a rabble-rouser." This recalls Paul's (unnamed) personal

Paulus should have shared the magnificent Macedonian spoils with them.[129] Since the latter were so numerous, the soldiers expected much more and complained of not receiving their share (34,7).[130] Marcus Servilius, a fellow consul, then defended Paulus in Rome before the soldiers, in part by telling them: "Although he might have made you rich by dividing the spoil, he is planning to carry the royal treasure in his triumph and deposit it in the treasury" (37,10). This Paulus then did when the three-day triumphal procession was completed.[131]

Plutarch considered it "worthy of admiration in Aemilius that, although he had subdued so great a kingdom [Macedonia], he did not add one drachma to his substance, nor would he touch or even look upon the conquered treasure; and yet he made liberal gifts to others."[132] He died so poor that his sons even had to sell some of Paulus' household goods, slaves and property in order to pay his wife's dowry.[133]

The fiscal propriety of Paulus, called into question by an individual, who incited others to think likewise, turned out to be unimpeachable. This recalls Paul's having to defend himself against the allegation of taking (financial) advantage of the Corinthians in 2 Cor 7:2 and 12:16-18, which is perhaps connected to the personal enemy alluded to in 2:5 and 7:12. Yet just as Paulus with the help of a fellow consul succeeded in asserting his fiscal propriety by devoting all the spoils of Macedonia in part to the Temple of Jupiter, but primarily to the city treasury, so Paul appears to have succeeded in becoming reconciled with his personal enemy and in maintaining that the entire sum of money he collected was indeed for the poor saints in Jerusalem and Judea, and not at all for him personally. Like that of Paulus, his fiscal propriety was unimpeachable.

---

enemy in the Corinthian congregation in 2 Cor 2:5 and 7:12, who caused him pain. For a similar situation of soldiers' wanting to raise a tumult and impede their victorious general's triumph because they had not received as much as expected, see Plutarch, "Pompey" 14,5.

[129] They maintained this in spite of their afterwards being allowed to take the booty of cities in Epirus (45.34,1-6).

[130] Cf. Plutarch, "Aemilius Paulus" 30,4 on the soldiers' having "cast longing eyes upon the royal treasures, since they had not got so much as they thought they deserved...."

[131] *Ibid.*, 38,1.

[132] Cf. the "Comparison of Timoleon and Aemilius" 2,8, and "Aemilius Paulus" 4,4-5. See also Dio Cassius 20 from Zonaras 9,24: "he scorned money."

[133] Cf. Polybius 18.35,4-8 and 31.22,4. The great avarice of Paulus' military opponent, King Perseus of Macedonia, was the exact opposite. See for example 29.8,2 and Plutarch, "Aemilius Paulus" 8,10.

6. Family Pedigree

Paul's opponents in Second Corinthians were also Jewish Christians like himself. Among other things they boasted (see section 7. below on this) of their credentials, apparently bringing along letters of recommendation from the mother church in Jerusalem (3:1). In addition, Paul asks in 11:22 :

> Are they Hebrews? So am I.
> Are they Israelites? So am I.
> Are they descendants of Abraham? So am I.

The remains of an inscription have been found in Corinth which can be reconstructed as "[Syn]agogue of the Hebr[ews]."[134] "Hebrew" and "descendant [seed] of Abraham" designate Jews from the point of race or ethnicity, while "Israelite" emphasizes the religious aspect. Paul is here putting himself on the same level as these Jewish-Christian "super-apostles" (11:5; 12:11) in regard to his ethnical and religious background. He could even have intensified this by mentioning, as he does elsewhere, that he was circumcised on the eighth day, a member of the tribe of Benjamin, and in regard to the law a Pharisee, extremely zealous for Jewish traditions.[135]

The Apostle may in part have also been inspired to relate his Jewish background in 2 Cor 11:22 because he is writing the epistle from Macedonia, where King Perseus, who had a distinguished pedigree, was defeated by Paul's namesake Paulus, himself from a fine family.

6.1 King Perseus

Livy in 45.7,3 relates regarding Perseus: "not only his reputation and that of his father, grandfather, and the rest to whom he was related by blood and stock made him a cynosure, but the glory of Philip and Alexander the Great, who made the Macedonians masters of the world, radiated from him." In 9,4 he then notes that the king had reigned eleven years "as the twentieth after Caranus, who had founded the kingdom."

---

[134] Cf. on this C. K. Barrett, *The Second Epistle to the Corinthians* 2 and 293. For Jews in Corinth at the time of Philo, see his *Leg. Gai.* 281, and Acts 18:4,7-8.
[135] Cf. Phil 3:5; Rom 11:1; and Gal 1:14.

6.2 Paulus

Plutarch writes that Paulus descended from the Aemilii, "one of the ancient and patrician houses at Rome," founded by Mamercus, a son of Pythagoras the philosopher. He "received the surname of Aemilius for the 'grace' (αἱμυλία)[137] and charm of his discourse." Lucius Paulus was a general who died bravely in battle at Cannae in Spain. His daughter Aemilia was married to Scipio the Great, and his son was Aemilius Paulus.[138]

The Apostle Paul, while born in Tarsus in the Diaspora (Acts 21:39 and 22:3), considered himself to be on the same level as or even superior to the "super-apostles," his Jewish-Christian opponents in Second Corinthians who were most probably from Jerusalem, the capital of the Jewish motherland. In his argumentation he may also have been thinking of how his namesake Paulus, whose pedigree was not as impressive as that of his opponent, King Perseus of Macedonia, a descendant of Philip and Alexander the Great, nevertheless conquered him and led him in a splendid, three-day triumphal procession through Rome. Paul was also confident of defeating his Jewish-Christian opponents in Corinth.

---

[136] Cf. his "Comparison of Timoleon and Aemilius" 1,2, and "Aemilius Paulus" 12,9; 27,4; and 31,5 for other references to his descent. Perseus' spurious birth as described in 8,11-12 of the latter is a later vilification.

[137] Cf. LSJ 39, who have "wheedling." The adjective αἱμύλος is "wheedling, wily," mostly of words. It is clear, however, that Plutarch means the noun positively, as in one case of αἱμύλιος. Cf. B. Perrin's reference to the adjective as meaning "winning" in a passage in the *Odyssey* ("Aemilius Paulus" 2,2, n. 2 in LCL 6.359).

[138] "Aemilius Paulus" 2,1-5. In 4,1-5 he is described as being sent as a praetor, but with consular dignity, to Spain (in 191 BCE) to quell an uprising there. He did so successfully, slaying ca. 30,000 of the enemy, mastering 250 cities, and bringing peace to the area. On Paulus' bringing back to Rome a large amount of gold on this occasion, yet not taking any of it for himself, see Polybius 31.22,3. For his father's dying at Cannae and the results for Rome, see Velleius Paterculus, *Compendium of Roman History* 1.9,3; William Reiter, *Aemilius Paullus* 109; and Polybius 5.105,10 and 111,8; 6.11,2 and 58,2.

7. Boasting and Weakness

Paul employs the related terms for "boasting," καυχάομαι, καύχημα and καύχησις, nine times in Romans,[139] ten times in First Corinthians, three times in Galatians, three times in Philippians, once in First Thessalonians, and ἐγκαυχάομαι once in 2 Thess 1:4.[140] Yet the Apostle uses them thirty times in Second Corinthians, from 1:12 to 12:9. In part this has to do with his very boastful opponents there.

Paul's Jewish-Christian missionary opponents "commend"[141] themselves with letters of recommendation, which he does not need (3:1). He and his co-workers do not "commend" themselves to the Corinthians again, but give them an opportunity to boast about them so that they can answer "those who boast in outward appearance and not in the heart" (5:12).[142] Paul and his co-workers in contrast "commended" themselves as servants of God, enduring great hardships (6:4-10; cf. 11:23-33). In contrast to their opponents, they will not boast beyond limits. This includes the labors of others (10:13,15), that is, "work already done in someone else's sphere of action" (v 16). The opponents seek an opportunity to be recognized as their "equals in what they boast about" (11:12), yet such [boasters] are "false apostles, deceitful workers, disguising themselves as apostles of Christ" (v 13). They boast according to the flesh, i.e. human standards (v 18). They make slaves of the Corinthians, prey upon them, and take [monetary] advantage of them, putting on airs (v 20), daring to boast that they are Hebrews, Israelites and descendants of Abraham (vv 21-22; cf. section 6. above). In contrast, Paul prefers paradoxically to boast of his weaknesses (11:30; 12:5,9). He knows that he, unlike the opponents, has the authority of the Lord (10:8; 13:10).

I suggest that Paul, writing to the Corinthians in Achaia from Macedonia, emphasized his general unwillingness to boast about his own exploits in part because he thought of his namesake Paulus' refusal to boast over King Perseus of Macedonia, who himself was a boaster.

---

[139] This includes the κατακαυχάομαι of Rom 11:18 (BAGD 411).
[140] Cf. BAGD 427-28 on the first three, and 216 on the latter, as well as the art. καυχάομαι , etc., by Rudolf Bultmann in *TDNT* 3.645-54. I myself think the authorship of Second Thessalonians should at least remain an open question. Therefore I cite it here and elsewhere along with the undisputed letters of Paul.
[141] Cf. BAGD 790,1.b., on συνιστάνω .
[142] Cf. 10:18 for the opponents' also commending themselves.

In an excerpt from Zonaras 9,24, Dio Cassius in his *Roman History* 20 notes that Perseus "boasted (ὁ...αὐχῶν)¹⁴³ of tracing his descent through twenty kings and often had on his lips the name of Philip and still oftener that of Alexander...."¹⁴⁴ This recalls the Jewish-Christian opponents of Paul in Corinth, who also boasted of their descent (2 Cor 11:22 in section 6. above).

After Perseus was defeated and captured, Paulus called a council, which included his sons and sons-in-law and young officers. Polybius in 29.20,1 notes that he then "exhorted those present at the council to learn from what they now witnessed – showing them Perseus who was present – never 'to boast unduly' (μεγαλαυχεῖν)¹⁴⁵ of achievements and never be overbearing and merciless in their conduct to anyone, in fact never place any reliance on present prosperity." In such moments one should rather "reflect on the opposite extremity of fortune" (20,2).¹⁴⁶ In his "Aemilius Paulus" 27, Plutarch also relates this speech, noting that he is here dependent on other, earlier sources (27,6). Paulus asked those present at the council: "Is it then fitting that one who is mortal should 'be emboldened'¹⁴⁷ when success comes to him, or 'have high thoughts'¹⁴⁸ because he has subdued a nation, or a city, or a kingdom? Or should his thoughts dwell rather on this reversal of fortune, which sets before the warrior an illustration of the 'weakness' (ἀσθένεια)¹⁴⁹ that is common to all men, and teaches him to regard nothing as stable or safe?" (27,2). Paulus admonishes the assembled young men to abandon "empty indolence" and the "arrogance"¹⁵⁰ of victory. Rather, they should take a humble posture in light of how fate could reverse itself. Paulus then dismissed the young men with their "excessive boasting" (μάλα τὸ καύχημα) and hubris, having curbed them by using cutting words in his speech, "as by a bridle" (27,5-6).¹⁵¹ Finally, Dio

---

¹⁴³ Cf. LSJ 285 on αὐχέω : boast, plume oneself.
¹⁴⁴ Cf. LCL 2.354-55.
¹⁴⁵ Cf. LSJ 1086: boast, brag. The LCL translator, W. R. Paton, correctly adds "unduly" because of the μεγαλ-.
¹⁴⁶ Cf. Livy 45.8,6 with "fortune" and "misfortune" (*adversae*).
¹⁴⁷ Cf. LSJ 804 on θρασύνω : "embolden; 2. w. acc. boast of."
¹⁴⁸ Cf. LSJ 1956, 2.b. on the phrase μέγα φρονεῖν in the bad sense of "to be presumptuous."
¹⁴⁹ LSJ 256: want of strength, weakness.
¹⁵⁰ Cf. LSJ 339 on γαυρίαμα . A γαύρηξ is a braggart, and γαύρωμα is a subject for boasting.
¹⁵¹ Cf. also Diodorus of Sicily 30.23,1 with not boasting (μήτε μέγα λέγειν) in this context.

Cassius notes in 67,2 that Paulus "did not assume a pompous or 'boastful' attitude toward Perseus."[152]

Paulus' refusal to boast over someone who himself boasted of his lineage, and his emphasis on the "weakness" common to all men, may in part have inspired his namesake, the Apostle Paul, to boast paradoxically only of his "weaknesses" in contrast to his opponents' boasting of their own lineage. In addition, a Roman general victorious on the battlefield then had to convince the Senate that he deserved a triumphal procession through the city. To do this, he had to list his achievements, including the many hardships of the war.[153] This too could have inspired Paul, who envisages God as leading him and his co-workers in a triumphal procession in 2 Cor 2:14, to list the many hardships encountered in his ministry in 4:8-12; 6:4-10; 11:23-33; and 12:10. It is these weaknesses which he would rather boast about (12:9; cf. 11:18).

8. Consolation

The verb παρακαλέω is used eighteen times in Second Corinthians, and the noun παράκλησις [154] eleven times, making a total of twenty-nine times. Elsewhere they occur much less frequently in the Pauline Corpus,[155] showing Paul's great emphasis on these terms in this particular letter. Of the eighteen times they clearly mean here to console / comfort, consolation / comfort, fifteen are found in 1:3-7 and 7:5-7.[156] The latter is often thought to begin a new section which takes up the thought ending in 2:13.

Otto Schmitz calls 2 Cor 1:3-7 part of "the great chapter of comfort in the NT."[157] It deserves to be quoted fully.

---

[152] Cf. LSJ 60, II. 3 on the adj. ἀλάζων : boastful.
[153] Cf. for example Dionysius of Halicarnassus, *Ant.* 6.30,2; Livy 26.21,2-6 and 31,7 ("many hardships on land and sea"); 28.28,2-4; 37.46,2-3 and 59,2.
[154] Cf. BAGD 617-18; the article on these two terms by Otto Schmitz and Gustav Stählin in *TDNT* 5.773-99, esp. 797-98; and C. J. Bjerkelund, *Parakalô. Form, Funktion und Sinn der parakalô-Sätze in den paulinischen Briefen* (Oslo: Universitetsforlaget, 1967).
[155] Cf. nine times in First Thessalonians, seven times each in Romans and First Corinthians, and three times each in Philippians, Second Thessalonians and Philemon.
[156] Elsewhere, only 2 Thess 2:16 and 17 clearly have the meaning of comfort. Other passages convey encourage / -ment, which, however, is closely associated.
[157] Cf. *TDNT* 5.797-98.

> Blessed be the God and Father of our Lord Jesus Christ, the Father of mercies and the God of all consolation, 4) who consoles us in all our affliction, so that we may be able to console those who are in any affliction with the consolation with which we ourselves are consoled by God. 5) For just as the sufferings of Christ are abundant for us, so also our consolation is abundant through Christ. 6) If we are being afflicted, it is for your consolation and salvation; if we are being consoled, it is for your consolation, which you experience when you patiently endure the same sufferings that we are also suffering. 7) Our hope for you is unshaken; for we know that as you share in our sufferings, so also you share in our consolation.

Here the God of all consolation consoles Paul and his co-workers with consolation in all their "affliction" (θλῖψις) so that they in turn can console others in a similar situation, including "sufferings" (παθήματα) on the part of both, similar to Christ's sufferings.

Paul's great emphasis on to console / comfort and consolation / comfort here may in part be due to his having in mind how his namesake, Paulus, after a major military victory in Macedonia (from where Paul is writing), tried to comfort others in his own situation of weakness.

Paulus had two sons by his first wife, whom he divorced. These he had adopted into illustrious families.[158] His second wife bore him two sons, whom he purposely kept at home to become his heirs. Livy relates that "the younger boy, aged about twelve, died five days before the triumph, and the elder, fourteen years old, died three days after the festival" (45.40,7).

Several days after his triumphal procession Paulus held a speech at an assembly of the commons, "as was customary for commanders, on his exploits" (40,9). Here, directly after his triumph and his sons' funerals, he compared his own fortune with that of the state. In light of the good fortune (*fortuna*) he enjoyed in the Macedonian war, he feared a negative change. His hope was that "the brunt of this change should not fall upon the state, but upon my household" (41,8). He concluded his address by stating: "Not a Paulus is left in my house, save an old man. But 'I am consoled' (*consolatur*) in this 'disaster' (*clades*) to my house by your 'happiness' (*felicitas*) and the good 'fortune' (*fortuna*) of the state."

---

[158] They were Quintus Fabius Maximus and Publius Scipio, who also accompanied him in the Macedonian campaign. Cf. Livy 44.35,14 and 44,2, as well as Plutarch, "Aemilius Paulus" 5,1 and 5.

In his "Aemilius Paulus" 36, Plutarch, dependent here on earlier sources (37,1), relates the same scene. He notes that Paulus spoke to the Roman people "as a man who did not ask for 'comfort' (παραμυθία), but rather sought 'to comfort' (παραμυθέομαι)[159] his fellow-citizens in their distress over his own misfortunes" (36,2). In spite of his sons' deaths, he stated: "I am in no peril of what most concerned me, and I am confident, and I think that Fortune (τύχη) will remain constant to our city and do her no harm. For that deity has sufficiently used me and 'my afflictions' (τοῖς ἐμοῖς κακοῖς) to satisfy the divine displeasure at our successes, and she makes the hero of the triumph as clear an example of human 'weakness' (ἀσθενεία) as the victim of the triumph; except that Perseus, even though conquered, has his children, while Aemilius, though conqueror, has lost his" (36,8-9).[160]

Here Paulus, in spite of his own "loss," "misfortunes" and "afflictions," making him an example of human "weakness," nevertheless tries to "console" others. This behavior became a model for later writers on the subject of grief and consolation.[161] It is thus quite possible that the Apostle Paul also in part had Paulus' situation in mind, a combination of affliction / weakness, triumph and consolation, when he composed his major section on consolation in affliction and sufferings in 2 Cor 1:3-7, with the imagery of triumph following shortly thereafter in 2:14.

---

[159] On these expressions as also meaning comfort / consolation and to console / comfort, cf. BAGD 620 and LSJ 1318. Paul employs the noun together with παράκλησις in 1 Cor 14:3 and Phil 2:1 (as παραμύθιον), and the verb with παρακαλῶ in 1 Thess 2:12 and 5:14.

[160] Cf. also Appian, "Macedonian Affairs" 19, as well as Diodorus of Sicily 31.11,1-3, with being deeply grieved.

[161] Cf. for example Cicero, "Tusculan Disputations" 3,28 (70-71) in LCL XVIII 308-09, referring to his own *In Consolatione,* and Valerius Maximus, *Memorable Doings and Sayings* 5.10,2 on Aemilius Paulus, who is "the most famous model of a very happy father suddenly turned very miserable." In this section (10), "Of Parents who Bore the Death of their Children with Fortitude," he is the second of three examples. On the Greco-Roman consolation tradition, see also the many references in Abraham Malherbe, *The Letters to the Thessalonians* (AB 32B; New York: Doubleday, 2000) 152, 276 and 278-81, as well as in "On the genre of Philippians: ancient consolation," in Paul Holloway, *Consolation in Philippians: Philosophical Sources and Rhetorical Strategy* (SNTSMS 112; Cambridge: Cambridge University Press, 2001) 55-83.

9. The "Ovatio," and a Triumph Through Persuasion

In the various parts of Second Corinthians the Apostle Paul emphasizes numerous times that his type of evangelization is by persuasion. The Corinthians' contribution to Paul's collection for the poor saints in Jerusalem / Judea, for example, should not be thought of as the result of a command from him (8:8), neither as an extortion nor as done under compulsion, but as a voluntary gift (9:6-7). He intentionally does not take personal remuneration from them for his ministry (11:7-9) so that he can appear more credible. His behavior and speech are "with frankness and sincerity" (1:12; 2:17), not with cunning (4:2). He also states in the latter verse that "by the open statement of the truth we commend ourselves to the conscience of everyone in the sight of God."[162] In 5:11 he remarks: "knowing the fear of God, 'we try to persuade' (πείθομεν) others."[163] He and his co-workers "are ambassadors" for Christ, with God making His appeal through them (5:20). Employing martial imagery in 10:4-5, Paul also states: "We destroy 'arguments' (λογισμούς) and every proud obstacle raised up against the knowledge of God, and we take every 'thought' (νόημα) captive to obey Christ."[164] Paul's ministry can thus correctly be called one of persuasion.

In characterizing his ministry in such terms, the Apostle, who employed the image of a triumphal procession in 2:14, may be thinking of himself in terms of a particular kind of triumph. In addition to the *triumphus* there existed the *ovatio*.[165] It differed from the *triumphus* by the victorious general's entering Rome not in a chariot, but on foot, sometimes but not always followed by his army,[166] and wearing "a wreath of the myrtle of Venus Victrix," thus not of laurel as in a *triumphus*.[167] In addition, according to Plutarch, "Marcellus" 22,2, the

---

[162] On the motif of truth, cf. also 6:7; 7:14; and 13:8.
[163] Cf. πείθω in BAGD 639.
[164] On λογισμός , cf. BAGD 476-77, and 540 on νόημα .
[165] Cf. the art. "Ovatio" by G. Rohde in PW (1942) 36.1,1890-1903, and the short art. by Christian Gizewski in *Der neue Pauly* (2000) 9.110, who cites the relevant discussions in Versnel, *Triumphus*, and Künzl, *Der römische Triumph*. The other two kinds of triumph, that on the Alban Mount (see for example Livy 42.21,7) and the naval triumph, are irrelevant here.
[166] Cf. the sources cited by Rohde, "Ovatio" 36.1, 1899-1900.
[167] Cf. Pliny, *Natural History* 15,125 and 127 on the two types of wreath. For a general's entry on foot, followed by the army, see for example Dionysius of Halicarnassus, *Ant.* 5.47,3, who also describes his wearing different clothing, "but everything else is the same."

victorious general celebrating an *ovatio* was "accompanied by the sound of exceeding many flutes."[168] The use of this musical instrument in the *ovatio* may have reminded the Apostle Paul of its use in the festal procession of those bringing first-fruits to the Temple in Jerusalem (see section 4. above).

The *ovatio* was awarded by the Senate for a general's winning a "dustless" and bloodless victory, for example by the opponent's surrendering,[169] and for ending a war through a treaty.[170] Plutarch in "Marcellus" 22,3-4 notes, however, that "to those generals who had no need of war, but had brought everything to a good issue 'by means of conference, persuasion, and argument' (ὁμιλίᾳ δὲ καὶ πειθοῖ καὶ διὰ λόγου), the law awarded the privilege of conducting, like a paean of thanksgiving, this unwarlike and festal procession. For the flute is an instrument of peace, and the myrtle is a plant of Aphrodite, who more than all the other gods abhors violence and wars." This θρίαμβος is the *ovatio*.[171]

Paul himself may have been aware of the emperor Caligula's celebrating an *ovatio* in 40 CE[172] and of Aulus Plautius' doing so in 47 CE.[173] In his *Natural History* 15,19, Pliny notes that not only the victorious general, but also the cavalry squadrons following him, wearing olive wreaths, can be designated as *ovantes*,[174] i.e. they triumph together with the general. Along with my interpretation above of θριαμβεύω in 2 Cor 2:14 as implying God the Lord of hosts' leading Paul and his co-workers in a triumphal procession as if they were his officers,

---

[168] This was in contrast to the use of trumpets in the *triumphus*. Cf. the many sources cited for the latter in Ehlers, "Triumphus" 13.503. See for example Diodorus of Sicily 31.8,10 on Aemilius Paulus' triumphal procession: "as in war, trumpeters led the way."
[169] Cf. *The Attic Nights of Aulus Gellius* 5.6,20-23, who states that such a *triumphus* was not of Mars, but of Venus; Pliny, *Natural History* 15,125; Isidore, "De Triumphis" in his *Etymologiarum* 18,2, quoting Sallustius, *Hist.* 3,29; and Ovid, "The Amores" 2,12.
[170] Cf. for example Dionysius of Halicarnassus, *Ant.* 9.36,3 with τὸν πέζον θρίαμβον ; and Livy 10.37,4 and 9.
[171] Plutarch then attempts a very questionable etymology of the word; cf. n. 1 in LCL 5.497.
[172] Cf. Suetonius, "Caligula" 49,2.
[173] Cf. Suetonius, "Claudius" 24,3, which states that the emperor accompanied him on foot during the entire procession. See also the other sources cited by Rohde, "Ovatio" 36.1, 1903, and for the dates 1902-03.
[174] This is noted by Rohde, "Ovatio" 36.1, 1892.

this usage of *ovatio* - *ovantes* may also have encouraged Paul to think in this direction.

The *ovatio* was regarded as a completely valid triumph, and was also translated into Greek as θρίαμβος (like the verb *ovo* as θριαμβεύω), making it at least in this respect indistinguishable from the Latin *triumphus*. The *ovatio* would also have appealed to the Apostle Paul because it did not involve killing at least 5000 enemy soldiers, but was bloodless. In addition, to my knowledge it is not known that the general celebrating this kind of triumph painted his face red with *minium* or cinnebar, as was done in the *triumphus*, and to the face of Jupiter's statue in his temple on the Capitol, the end of the procession. This usage may have been originally connected to the color of blood shed in the war.[175] As a Jew Paul would also have viewed with disapproval the custom of hanging a large phallus under the chariot of the general celebrating a *triumphus*. As with its being tied around the necks of infants, it was here considered to be apotropaic, i.e. to ward off evil.[176] The chariot was also lacking in the *ovatio*, where the triumphator went on foot. Finally, the awarding of an *ovatio*, a form of triumph including a procession through Rome, on the basis of a Roman general's "persuading" an enemy by argumentation to surrender and make peace, would greatly have appealed to the Apostle, who himself conducted a ministry of persuading others in regard to the Gospel. Paul and his co-workers, like the officers of such a general, are represented in 2 Cor 2:14 as being led by God, the Lord of hosts, in a similar procession.

---

[175] On the usage, cf. Pliny, *Natural History* 33,111.157. While the origin is unclear, at least Dio Cassius favored the latter theory. See his excerpt from Tzetzes, Epist. 107, p. 86 in LCL 1.194-95.

[176] Cf. Pliny, *Natural History* 28,39 on "Fascinus": "hanging under the chariots of generals at their triumphs, he defends them as a physician from jealousy, and the similar physic of the tongue bids them look back, so that at the back Fortune, destroyer of fame, may be won over." See also the art. by E. Kuhnert, "Fascinum," in PW (1909) 6.2009-14, esp. 2011, line 32, to 2012, line 28, with the connection to the cult of Liber (Dionysos). On the latter, see the art. "Liber, Liberalia" by Francesca Prescendi in *Der neue Pauly* (1999) 7.136-37, and the art. "Dionysos" by O. Kern in PW (1905) 5.1042, lines 9-37. For a whip and a bell as also attached to the chariot in order to indicate to the triumphator "that it was possible for him to meet with misfortune also, to the extent even of being scourged or condemned to death," see Dio Cassius 6 from Zonaras 7,21 (LCL 1.198-99).

10. No Triumph for Fighting in Another's Province

In Jerusalem Paul had been entrusted with the Gospel for the uncircumcised, i.e. the Gentiles (Gal 2:7-9; cf. Acts 15). In 2 Corinthians 10, the Apostle states that in contrast to his Jewish-Christian opponents, probably outfitted with letters of recommendation from Jerusalem (3:1), he (and his co-workers) will not boast beyond limits. Rather, "we will keep within the field that God has assigned to us, to reach out even as far as you [Corinthians]. For we were not overstepping our limits when we reached you; we were the first to come all the way to you with the good news of Christ. We do not boast beyond limits, that is, in the labors of others; but our hope is that, as your faith increases, our sphere of action among you may be greatly enlarged, so that we may proclaim the good news in lands beyond you, without boasting of work already done in someone else's sphere of action" (10:13-16).

That Paul felt very strongly about the issue of such limits is shown in Rom 15:20-21. There he states: "I make it my ambition to proclaim the good news, not where Christ has already been named, so that I do not build on someone else's foundation." He then quotes LXX Isa 52:15 to support his policy in regard to mission field limits.[177]

I suggest that Paul developed his thinking in regard to not entering someone else's already established field of mission in part because of his awareness of a convention connected to the awarding of a triumph. Livy for example notes in 34.10,3 that Marcus Helvius, the governor of Farther Spain, was not granted a triumph: "The reason for the senate's refusal of a triumph was that he had fought under another's auspices and in another's province."[178] Another instance is found in 28.9,10. This usage could very well have influenced Paul's fierce independence, not wanting to conduct his ministry to the Gentiles in someone else's (mission) territory. In regard to his perception of his own mission field, he thought that God, the Lord of hosts, here led him and his co-workers, and only them, in His triumphal procession (2 Cor 2:14).

---

[177] Cf. 16:1 and 23 (see also 1 Cor 1:14) for Romans as most probably written in Corinth.
[178] He nevertheless was later granted an *ovatio*: 34.10,5-6.

11. The Meaning of θριαμβεύω in 2 Cor 2:14

Paul Duff spoke of τῷ ... ἡμᾶς in 2 Cor 2:14a as a "striking and enigmatic phrase," whose significance is "far from clear."[179] For this reason so many possible meanings have been proposed for it. My suggestion as described above is that Paul, in Macedonia and thinking of the well-known triumphal procession through Rome of his namesake Paulus after his stunning victory over King Perseus in Macedonia, first thanks God (χάρις). This was customarily done at the end of the procession, in the Temple of Jupiter on the Capitol. The object ("us") of God's "leading in triumph" is Paul and his co-workers, such as Timothy (1:1 and 18) and Silvanus (1:18; cf. Acts 18:5 with Silas and Timothy). It is they whom God, the Lord of "hosts," leads as His major officers in triumph, just as a triumphator led his officers behind or next to him in the triumphal procession, celebrating his major military victory. As shown in one example of θριαμβεύω in Appian, one of *triumphantes* in Livy, and one of *ovantes* in Pliny, the officers and or soldiers could be thought of as sharing in the general's triumph. Paul's use of warfare imagery later in this epistle, and of his "fellow soldiers" in other letters, strengthens this proposal. The term θριαμβεύω is thus to be understood *positively*,[180] according with the initial "thanksgiving" and the following

---

[179] Cf. his "Metaphor, Motif, and Meaning: The Rhetorical Strategy behind the Image 'Led in Triumph' in 2 Corinthians 2:14" in *CBQ* 53 (1991) 79. C. K. Barrett in *The Second Epistle to the Corinthians* 97 with English understatement had earlier remarked: "The meaning is not perfectly clear." Alfred Plummer even earlier noted that of the expressions Paul uses to describe himself as a minister of the Gospel, "this metaphor...is the most striking of all." See his *Second Epistle of St Paul to the Corinthians* 68. Hans-Josef Klauck in *2. Korintherbrief* (Neue Echter Bibel; Würzburg: Echter Verlag, 1986) 32 speaks of "der nicht leicht zu durchschauenden Bildersprache" here. Paul Barnett in *The Second Epistle to the Corinthians* (NICNT; Grand Rapids, Michigan: Eerdmans, 1997) 147 can also state: "The sudden [δὲ] and unheralded introduction of triumphal imagery is striking." Regina Plunkett-Downing in *Reading and Restoration* 37 speaks of "the opaque metaphor" of the triumph. In contrast, Heinz-Dietrich Wendland in *Die Briefe an die Korinther* 152 could comment on it as "dem schönen kraftvollen Bild vom Triumphator," and M. Margareta Gruber in *Herrlichkeit in Schwachheit. Eine Auslegung der Apologie des Zweiten Korintherbriefes, 2 Kor 2,14 - 6,13* (Forschung zur Bibel 89; Würzburg: Echter, 1998) 105 as "der kühnen Triumphmetapher." She deals on pp. 97-146 with the pericope.

[180] Cf. Hans Windisch's statement that one would expect after χάρις something about the successes for which the Apostles should thank God: *Der zweite Korintherbrief* 96. See also Margaret Thrall, *The Second Epistle to the Corinthians*,

φανεροῦντι δι' ἡμῶν ἐν παντὶ τόπῳ, "making known through us in every place" the fragrance that comes from knowing Christ, a reference to the apostles' (pl.) spreading the Gospel or "good news" in the Mediterranean area.[181] The "always" may be a veiled allusion to contemporary emperors' maintaining the state ideology of "eternal triumph." The above relatively infrequent[182] meaning of θριαμβεύω by Paul, metaphorical as in other contemporary writers, also helps explain the following imagery in vv 15-16 of fragrance and aroma. Incense was not only carried in the triumphal procession. It also played a major role in the sacrifices of thanksgiving at the end of such a procession, where wine poured on incense, increasing its fragrance, was offered at the sacrifice of every ox or other animal to Jupiter.

In addition, Paul's having the triumph of Paulus over Macedonia in mind may also, in addition to other factors, have influenced his setting up centers for the gathering of financial contributions to his "collection"; his defense of his fiscal propriety; his citing his descent; his boasting only of weakness; the motif of consolation in affliction; emphasis on his use of persuasion to gain converts, similar to a form of the Roman triumph also awarded for a victory through persuasion; and his unwillingness to do mission work in another's area or province since a triumph was not granted for such activity.

If the above presentation is basically correct, it means that a number of other views of the meaning of θριαμβεύω in 2 Cor 2:14 in its context should be modified.

1. Rudolf Bultmann thought that the context of 2:14-17 was lost and that a later redactor inserted the passage at this point.[183] Ralph Martin

---

Volume I, Chapters 1-7 (ICC; Edinburgh: Clark, 1994) 192: "This would make good sense...."

[181] Cf. the statement by T. W. Manson in "2 Corinthians 2 14-17: Suggestions towards an exegesis," in *Studia Paulina in honorem Johannis de Zwaan*, ed. J. N. Sevenster and W. C. van Unnik (Harlem: Bohn, 1953) 161: God "carries us along in the victorious progress of the Messianic triumph, which is sweeping through the world."

[182] Cf. Lamar Williamson, Jr., in "Led in Triumph. Paul's Use of *Thriambeuō*" in *Int* 22 (1968) 323: "A fertile mind can and often does give new dimensions to a word." This is true if one admits that Paul employs the verb in a manner seldom used by others: he "renews" its meaning in this sense.

[183] Cf. his *Der zweite Brief an die Korinther* (Meyer; Vandenhoeck & Ruprecht, 1976) 66. The view of Jean-François Collange is similar. See his *Énigmes de la deuxiéme épître de Paul aux Corinthiens*: Étude exégétique de 2 Cor 2:14 - 7:4 (SNTSMS 18; Cambridge: Cambridge University Press, 1972) 23 and 40. See also

considers v 14 to be possibly redactional, "the opening of a letter originally independent and added in here when the fragments of 2 Corinthians were assembled."[184] Yet 2:14-17 are indeed from Paul, triggered by the previous catchword Macedonia and the triumph over Macedonia by Paul's namesake Paulus, one of the most magnificent and longest (three-day) triumphal processions ever to have taken place.

2. Frederick Field dismisses here "all reference to the Roman triumph."[185] Victor Furnish also has his doubts in this regard.[186] However, the sources cited above in sections 1.-10. all argue against this. Paul indeed alludes to the Roman triumphal procession in 2:14, although in a relatively infrequent, metaphorical manner.

3. George Findlay suggested already in 1882 that θριαμβεύω here means "*to lead in festal or choral (dithrambic) procession, to lead in triumph*" "as the inspiring Deity his exultant worshippers."[187] Paul Duff's more general view, that an epiphany procession is alluded to here, is similar.[188] Yet as Duff concedes, the triumphal procession is a sub-category of the *pompa* / πομπή. Aspects of other Greco-Roman processions should only be considered of direct relevance to 2 Cor 2:14-17 if they are close to the imagery contained there, for example in regard to incense, as I pointed out in section 2.2 above.

4. In 1910 Arthur Kinsey argued for the "hiphil sense of θριαμβεύω - 'causeth us to triumph,'" asking: "May not the Christian be regarded as the honoured friend of the great Victor, asked to accompany Him in the

---

the view of Hans Dieter Betz cited in n. 3 of the Introduction. M. Margareta Gruber in *Herrlichkeit in Schwachheit* 116 and 119 speaks of 2:14 as beginning the entire letter of 2:14 – 6:13.

[184] Cf. his *2 Corinthians* (WBC 40; Waco, TX: Word Books, 1986) 45, building upon Collange and Bornkamm.

[185] Cf. his *Notes on the Translation of the New Testament* (Cambridge: Cambridge University Press, 1899) 181.

[186] Cf. his *II Corinthians* (AB 32A; Garden City, NY: Doubleday, 1984) 175: "one cannot be completely certain that Paul intends an allusion to the Roman triumph."

[187] Cf. his "St. Paul's Use of ΘΡΙΑΜΒΕΥΩ" in *The Expositor* 10 (1882) 416. He refers especially to "the mystic Dionysiac triumph," which has been Christianized here (420).

[188] Cf. his "Metaphor, Motif, and Meaning" 82-86, referring to Dionysius, Isis, Serapis, Anubis and Horus.

triumphal car, and share with Him the triumph-joy?"[189] Aside from the fact that the triumphator only allowed his minor children to ride with him in the chariot, Kinsey's proposal is based only on a Latin translation by Beza (d. 1605 CE). I suggest that the latter probably has this from Augustine (d. 430 CE).[190] If Kinsey had narrowed his suggestion to mean Paul and his co-workers as walking behind or beside the triumphal chariot, it would have been somewhat similar to my own proposal.

5. Scott Hafemann maintains that in 2:14a "Paul is rejoicing primarily because God, like a victorious general after his victory, is leading him as a *slave to death*!"[191] Although not stated so drastically, this view is also held by Hans-Josef Klauck,[192] Jens Schröter,[193] Arthur Kinsey,[194] Paul Duff,[195] and M. Margarete Gruber.[196] While it has solid lexical support, it

---

[189] Cf. his "The Triumph-Joy" in *ExpTim* 21 (1910) 282.
[190] For Beza, see his *Qui facit ut semper triumphemus in Christo* (Kinsey, *ibid.*). He probably is dependent on Augustine here, who interprets: "Now thanks be to God, who makes us triumph in Christ...." See his "Predestination of the Saints" 20,41 in *Ancient Christian Commentary on Scripture*, VII 209, and the Latin *qui semper triumphare nos facit in Christo* in *Aurelius Augustinus. Schriften gegen die Semipelagianer*, Vol. VII, with "Die Vorherbestimmung der Heiligen," 320.
[191] Cf. his *Suffering and the Spirit*. An Exegetical Study of II Cor. 2:14 - 3:3 within the Context of the Corinthian Correspondence (WUNT, 2.19; Tübingen: Mohr Siebeck, 1986) 35. This presupposes "Paul's prior defeat, i.e. his conversion-call on the road to Damascus, although not explicitly referred to" (p. 34). Joachim Kügler in "Paulus und der Duft" 167 correctly criticizes the latter view, although he nevertheless views Paul here as a slave (perhaps holding the incense) in the exalted Christ's triumphal procession (172-73).
[192] Cf. his *2. Korintherbrief* 32: "God leads Paul as a *prisoner* in the triumphal procession of Christ."
[193] Cf. his *Der versöhnte Versöhner. Paulus als unentbehrlicher Mittler im Heilvorgang zwischen Gott und Gemeinde nach 2 Kor 2,14 - 7,4* (TANZ 10; Tübingen and Basle: Francke, 1992) 13-31, esp. 17, yet he warns on p. 19 against over-emphasizing this aspect, and on p. 21 suggests simply God's triumphing "in regard to Paul," with an allusion to his calling. He then states on p. 22: "Wenn Gott jetzt also seinen Triumph feiert, so bedeutet dies, daß er den bei Damaskus besiegten und bekehrten Paulus nunmehr dazu benutzt, das Evangelium in der Welt zu verbreiten."
[194] Cf. his "The Triumph-Joy" 282: "the Damascus journey has transformed the enemy of Christ into His willing captive...."
[195] Cf. his "Metaphor, Motif and Meaning" 79. Yet Paul "is in fact a captive of the 'love of Christ,'" he "has been captured, not as a prisoner of war, but as a devotee of the deity." Cilliers Breytenbach in "Paul's Proclamation" 265 emphasizes in regard to θριαμβεύω : "the function can only be in the role of one of those

must be rejected because of its extremely negative character, which fits neither the χάρις thanksgiving directly before it, labeled "a paean of praise" by R. H. Strachen,[197] nor the positive meaning of what directly follows: "making known through us in every place," that is, proclaiming the "good news." It also does not allow for the possibility of Paul's employing a relatively infrequent, yet attested metaphorical usage of θριαμβεύω.

6. The latter positive interpretation also argues against those scholars who see the verb as a metaphor of social shame: Peter Marshall[198] and Victor Furnish.[199]

7. Other interpreters prefer here the meaning of "to make known publicly,"[200] "to lead about publicly,"[201] "which always makes a show (or spectacle) of us,"[202] and "making us known."[203] This, however, interprets the meaning of the verb directly following, φανερόω, "to reveal, make known, show,"[204] back into θριαμβεύω, and it denies an allusion to the Roman triumph, which is definitely referred to here.

---

conquered." For him this is not a captive led to his execution, but God's conquering Paul through the Damascus experience. Thus the verb "may have the sense 'to celebrate (by means of a triumph) a prior victory over somebody'" (p. 268). "Through Paul's proclamation of Christ, God, the victorious general, always celebrates his victory over Paul. He conquered Paul and now Paul spreads his fame" (p. 269). He is followed here by Jan Lambrecht, *Second Corinthians* (Sacra Pagina 8; Collegeville, MN: The Liturgical Press, 1999) 38-39.
[196] In *Herrlichkeit in Schwachheit* 104, she combines this with emphasis on being publicly presented in shame. See the following remarks in 6. and 7.
[197] Cf. his *The Second Epistle of Paul to the Corinthians* (Moffatt's; London: Hodder and Stoughton, 1935 / 1954) 73. See also F. F. Bruce, *1 and 2 Corinthians* 187: "a paean of thanksgiving."
[198] Cf. his "A Metaphor of Social Shame: ΘΡΙΑΜΒΕΥΕΙΝ in 2 Cor. 2:14" in *NovT* 25 (1983) 302-17.
[199] Cf. his *II Corinthians* 187, on the condition that the allusion is to a triumph.
[200] Cf. Rudolf Bultmann, *Der zweite Brief an die Korinther* 66, and Gerhard Dautzenberg, art. θριαμβεύω in *EWNT* 2.385.
[201] Cf. Hans Lietzmann, *An die Korinther I-II* 108.
[202] Cf. Frederick Field, *Notes* 181.
[203] Cf. Rory Egan, "Lexical Evidence on Two Pauline Passages" in *NovT* 19 (1977) 50, after noting the sense of "display, manifest, make known."
[204] BAGD 852.

Imagery of Triumph 45

8. While R. Martin Pope believes "the Apostle here conceives of God leading His subjugated saints in triumph, chained as captives to His car," their defeat consists in "the subduing of their rebellious passions and wills...."[205] Aside from the fact that captives in the triumphal procession were never chained to the triumphator's chariot, this allegorical interpretation sounds as if it could be by Philo of Alexandria. There is no indication of "subduing passions and wills" in the context.

9. Although Judaic mysticism, dealing with the interpretation of God's throne-chariot in Ezekiel 1, may provide some of the background for Paul's visions and revelations in 2 Cor 12:1-10, it exerts no recognizable influence in 2:14, as maintained by James Scott.[206]

10. There is also no evidence for the assertion of Dieter Georgi that θριαμβεύω is a term deriving from Paul's opponents.[207] Rather, as shown above, it derives from Paul himself, reminded at this point of his namesake Paulus' stunning victory in Macedonia and of his triumphal procession in Rome.

I have cited the above ten variant interpretations of θριαμβεύω in 2 Cor 2:14 in order to highlight my own explanation of it in its context. The color white is best perceived when set against various shades of gray up to black. I do not mean the latter in a triumphalistic way,[208] but as an honest attempt to emphasize the positive aspects of my own view.

---

[205] Cf. his "Studies in Pauline Vocabulary 1: of the Triumph-Joy" in *ExpTim* 21 (1910) 21.
[206] Cf. his "The Triumph of God in 2 Cor 2.14 : Additional Evidence of Merkabah Mysticism in Paul" in *NTS* 42 (1996) 260-81. I will deal more with this study later on in section II.
[207] Cf. his *The Opponents of Paul in Second Corinthians* (Edinburgh: Clark, 1987) 285, n. 29, borrowing from G. Bornkamm. He sees the Corinthians as a "strongly Gnostic community" (233), and six Gnostic motifs at work in vv 14-16 (285, n. 28). If my proposal above is basically correct, there is no reason at all to consider elements of Gnosticism to be reflected in these verses. See also Paul Duff, "Metaphor, Motif and Meaning" 82: "Paul alludes to the triumphal procession in 2:14 in order to characterize his opponents' claims about him."
[208] Cf. the remarks of Lamar Williamson, Jr., "Led in Triumph" 332 in regard to ecclesiastical, especially missionary triumphalism: "a proper understanding of Paul's use of *thriambeuō* condemns triumphalism in any part of the church." It is questionable, for example, why the hymn is still found in the *Lutheran Book of Worship* of 1978: "Onward, Christian soldiers, marching as to war," with "the

11. Finally, Regina Plunkett-Dowling's assertion that efforts to connect the imagery of triumph in 2:14a and the fragrances of 2:14b "seem strange and finally unpersuasive,"[209] is refuted by the sources cited above. They intimately connect the triumphal procession with extensive use of incense, producing such fragrances.[210]

* * *

The second source of Paul's imagery in 2 Cor 2:14-17, that of rebellion, remains to be analyzed.

---

triumph-song" in verse four. Any form of triumphalism today is rightfully suspect and counter-productive in regard to evangelism.
[209] Cf. her *Reading and Restoration* 37, n. 79.
[210] For the other major source of the fragrance / aroma imagery, see part II.

II. Judaic Imagery of Rebellion

Imagery from the Roman triumphal procession is not the only kind to have influenced 2 Cor 2:14-17. Paul, the converted Jew, here also drew upon imagery of rebellion from Judaic tradition on an OT passage well-known to him and to which he had already alluded in his first epistle to the Corinthians (see 8. below).

Not only an (unknown) individual had opposed the Apostle during his second visit to the Corinthians (2:5-11; 7:12). Others showed their rebellion towards the founder of their Christian congregation (10:14) by accusing him of "practicing cunning" and "falsifying God's word" (4:2, thus 2:17). In 12:16-18 Paul's opponents accuse him of being "crafty," of "taking [the Corinthians] in by deceit" (v 16). The latter have the strong suspicion that he is taking advantage of them by retaining for himself part of the collection ostensibly intended for the poor saints in Judea (chapters 8-9). He did this although he had refused any financial support from them while he was among them (11:7-9). In addition, so-called "super-apostles" encouraged rebellion towards Paul by maintaining that "his bodily presence is weak, and his speech contemptible" (10:10; cf. 11:5-6). The Apostle to the Gentiles thus sees himself forced to assert his authority (10:8; 13:10) in light of such open rebellion.

The above sketch helps to understand the short unit 2 Cor 2:14-17 better. It ends in v 17 by Paul's asserting that he and his helpers are not "peddlers of God's word like so many" – e.g., his opponents in Corinth. Rather, the Apostle and his fellow missionaries "in Christ speak as persons of sincerity, as persons sent from God and standing in His presence." This forceful assertion of his own authority in light of opposition and rebellion justifies asking whether an OT text dealing with rebellion, further developed in Judaic tradition, may have influenced Paul's thought and imagery in the pericope. I suggest that this was indeed the case.

One of the most famous rebellions or revolts in the Hebrew Bible is that of Korah, Dathan and Abiram in Numbers 16. Levites, they here seek the right to act as priests as well. They thus assemble with a group of 250 leaders of the congregation, confront Moses, and question his authority (along with that of Aaron). In order to have the issue decided by God, Moses tells them to take censers, put fire on them, and then lay incense on these before the Lord. God will then choose who is holy and will be allowed to approach Him. Korah and his company thus assemble at the entrance of the tent of meeting with their censers, fire and incense, and all are swallowed up by the earth, fire from the Lord consuming the 250 men offering the incense.[1]

Chapter 17:1-5 (Eng. 16:36-40) then states that no one of non-Aaronic descent may approach to offer incense before the Lord. Otherwise he will suffer the same fate as Korah and his company did, "just as the Lord had said to him through Moses" (17:5, Eng. 16:40).

The next unit, the conclusion of the incident (17:6-15, Eng. 16:41-50), is decisive for the interpretation of 2 Cor 2:14-17. It deals with further rebellion leading to the death of 14,700 Israelites.[2] It relates that the next day the whole congregation "murmured" (לון ,[3] γογγύζω [4]) against Moses and Aaron (v 6), which the NRSV appropriately translates as "rebelled," as in the targums *Onqelos, Pseudo-Jonathan* and *Neofiti 1*.[5] They maintain the two have caused the (unnecessary) death of the people of the Lord. When the congregation then assembles against them, Moses and Aaron go to the tent of meeting, where the Lord appears and speaks to Moses, telling him and Aaron to get away so that He can consume (the whole congregation) instantly. The two then fall on their faces (to assuage the Lord so that He will not take such a drastic measure), and Moses tells Aaron:

---

[1] Cf. the similar fate of Nadab and Abihu in Lev 10:1-3, even though they were Aaron's sons.

[2] In her *Reading and Restoration* 49-50, Regina Plunkett-Downing also briefly refers to the revolt of Korah and cites LXX Num 17:12-13 as the last of several possible sources for the image of fragrance in 2 Cor 2:14-17. Yet she is unaware of the Judaic development of the Numbers text. The most recent study of Moses in the NT also does not recognize this, only referring to 2 Corinthians 3. Cf. John Lierman, *The New Testament Moses*. Christian Perspectives of Moses and Israel in the Setting of Jewish Religion (WUNT 2.173; Tübingen: Mohr Siebeck, 2004) 167-72.

[3] BDB 534: murmur against.

[4] LSJ 355: mutter, murmur, grumble.

[5] Cf. Sperber, 1.251 on *Onqelos*; Rieder 2.218 on *Pseudo-Jonathan*; and Díez-Macho 4.161 on *Neofiti 1* (the *Fragment Targum* does not have the unit except for MS "V" on v 10); and Jastrow 1487 on רעם , ithpa.: 1) to be rebellious, to murmur.

11) "Take your censer, put fire on it from the altar and lay incense on it, and carry it quickly to the congregation and make atonement for them. For wrath has gone out from the Lord; the plague has begun."
12) So Aaron took it as Moses had ordered, and ran into the middle of the assembly, where the plague had already begun among the people. He put on the incense, and made atonement for the people.
13) He stood between the dead and the living; and the plague was stopped.
14) Those who died by the plague were 14,700, besides those who died in the affair of Korah.
15) When the plague was stopped, Aaron returned to Moses at the entrance of the tent of meeting.

The above verses, primarily 11-13, form part of the background of several images in 2 Cor 2:14-17, also in a context of Paul's dealing with a rebellious congregation. It will now be helpful in this regard to trace the development of Num 17:11-15 in seven different corpora of Judaic tradition, for it was primarily the latter from which the Apostle borrowed his imagery.[6] The relevance of each section to 2 Cor 2:14-17 will be pointed out in the section itself. Section 8. deals with 1 Cor 10:10,

---

[6] Paul obviously makes no overt quotation from these verses. To maintain that he "alludes" to them here can also be misleading if by an "allusion" one understands an indirect reference to a specific biblical term, phrase or verse, whereby the source is easily identifiable. That is also not the case here, otherwise commentators would have called attention to these verses (and only to them) before, which has not been done. Nevertheless, Paul does "allude" to them *via their development in Judaic tradition*. If one becomes aware of the latter, one can indeed recognize "allusions" to Num 17:6-15, primarily vv 12-13, in 2 Cor 2:14-16. Another appropriate term here would be "echo," as proposed by Richard Hays in *Echoes of Scripture in the Letters of Paul* (New Haven / London: Yale University Press, 1989). I appreciate, for example, his reference to "The poetic freedom with which Paul echoes Scripture..." (xiii), and his differentiation between an "allusion" as "used of obvious intertextual references, *echo* of subtler ones" (29). "Recurrence" is one of his seven tests for "hearing echoes" (29-32), and I consider it fulfilled in the subtle allusion or echo of *Judaic tradition* on Num 17:6-15 in 1 Cor 10:10 (see 8. below), and then in 2 Cor 2:14-16. The Gentile-Christian members of the Corinthian church(es) would clearly not have recognized the background of this imagery, and most of the Greek-speaking Jewish-Christian members only possibly. Yet people such as Crispus, the converted official of the Corinthian synagogue (Acts 18:8 and 1 Cor 1:14), could indeed have "heard" Judaic tradition on Num 17:6-15 (LXX 16:41-50) "echoed" here.

1. The Masoretic Text

a) The "censer" in Num 17:11 is the Hebrew מַחְתָּה ,[7] from the root חתה , "to snatch up," usually fire or coals.[8] It should be noted that the noun is also employed as a censer in Lev 16:12, where the (Aaronic) high priest on the Day of Atonement takes "a censer full of coals of fire from the altar before the Lord, and two handfuls of crushed sweet incense," to put them on the fire before the Lord in the Holy of Holies. The latter passage is important for the understanding of Wisd Sol 18:20-25 below, based in part on Num 17:11.

b) The Hebrew for "incense" in 17:11-12 is קְטֹרֶת , which can also mean "perfume,"[9] showing its sweet odor or fragrance. The noun is connected to (הַ)סַּמִּים , "spices,"[10] in numerous passages in the MT,[11] where the NRSV correctly translates "fragrant incense." The latter expression is not found in the LXX, which instead has τὸ θυμίαμα τῆς συνθέσεως, "compounded incense."[12] This is important to note in regard to the background of the terms ὀσμή and εὐωδία in 2 Cor 2:14-16. Here it suffices to observe that the latter mean "fragrance" / "odor," and "aroma," "fragrance" / "a fragrant odor," respectively.[13]

The Hebrew term בֹּשֶׂם , pl. בְּשָׂמִים , "spice," "perfume," "sweet odor,"[14] is mentioned as an ingredient of "fragrant incense" in Exod 25:6, 35:8 and 28.[15] "Fragrant incense with a sweet odor," seemingly redundant, is a possible translation of this, and not simply "spiced."

---

[7] BDB 367,3. Other passages have the meaning "snuff-holder" and "fire-pan."
[8] *Ibid.*
[9] BDB 882,2. and 3. respectively. Another meaning is 1., "sweet smoke of sacrifice." Exod 30:38 states that (incense produced for the Sanctuary) may not be misused as "perfume" (the hiphil of רִיחַ , "smell," "perceive odor," BDB 926: a denominative of the noun רֵיחַ , "scent," "odor").
[10] Cf. BDB 702 on סַם : *"spice,* used in incense," only in the plural.
[11] Cf. Exod 25:6; 30:7; 31:11; 35:8,15,28; 37:29; 39:38; 40:27; Lev 4:7; 16:12; Num 4:16; 2 Chron 2:3 and 13:11.
[12] Cf. LSJ 1716, I.g. on σύνθεσις : *"compounding* of essences and drugs."
[13] Cf. BAGD 586 and 329.
[14] BDB 141,1.
[15] Cf. also Exod 30:34 with the simple "incense."

This may in part have influenced Paul's choice of two separate but related terms, the ὀσμή and εὐωδία mentioned above. Finally, "fragrant incense" is closely connected to the "oil of anointing" in seven passages in Exodus,[16] and בְּשָׂמִים is also one of its ingredients.[17] Paul employs the term χρίω, "to anoint,"[18] only in 2 Cor 1:21, shortly before 2:14-17. It thus may have still been in the back of his mind when he employed the closely related expressions ὀσμή and εὐωδία in 2:14-16.

c) Num 17:11 states: "For 'wrath' has gone out from the Lord; the plague has begun." The Hebrew of "(the) wrath" here is הַקֶּצֶף.[19] Of the twenty-eight occurrences of this noun in the MT, it is only here determinate, i.e. with "the."[20] "The" wrath is probably already here thought of as an angel of destruction,[21] as is the case in later Judaic development of this verse (see below).

d) After Aaron put on the incense and atoned for the people, Num 17:13 states that "He stood between the dead and the living; and the plague was stopped." "The dead" (הַמֵּתִים), however, are not actually dead yet. They are "the dying," those already afflicted by the plague before Aaron's action.[22] Verse 14 then records their death. This is important to note in regard to later Judaic development of the passage, and above all in regard to Paul's employing this terminology in 2 Cor 2:15 ("among those who are being saved and among those who are perishing") and 16 ("to the one a fragrance from death to death, to the other a fragrance from life to life").

---

[16] Exod 25:6; 31:11; 35:8,15,28; 37:29; and 39:38.
[17] Cf. Exod 25:6; 30:23; 35:8 and 28.
[18] BAGD 887. The object of the aorist participle can refer to Paul and his fellow-workers, or to the baptized (implied in v 22). A wordplay is certainly intended in v 21: Χριστὸν καὶ χρίσας . The "Christ" was, of course, the "Anointed One," both in Greek and in Hebrew.
[19] Cf. BDB 893 on קֶצֶף .
[20] Also noted by Baruch Levine, *Numbers 1-20* (AB 4A; New York: Doubleday, 1993) 421: this indicates "that to the author it represented a known phenomenon."
[21] Cf. Jastrow 1406, who refers to this passage.
[22] Cf. Levine, *Numbers 1-20*, 420-21: "Here Aaron was positioned between those already stricken by the plague (the 'dead' of v 13) and those still unaffected (the 'living'). He waved the incense over the living, and it protected them from the advancing plague." See also section 7.3 below on this.

The above remarks on the MT of Num 17:6-15 help to understand the later Judaic interpretation of this major incident of rebellion against the authority of Moses. It culminated in Paul's appropriation of imagery from this *later interpretation* in 2 Cor 2:14-17.

2. The Septuagint

The LXX translation of the Pentateuch may go back to the third century BCE.[23] In Num 17:6-15 (16:41-50) a number of details change. Verse 6 lacks "whole" in "the whole congregation," which may be an attempt by the translator(s) to mitigate the degree of the congregation's rebellion against Moses. Verse 7 intensifies Moses' and Aaron's "turning" towards the tent of meeting through the choice of the verb ὁρμάω, which connotes "running headlong at."[24] It also anticipates the "quickly" of v 11. Verse 9 adds "and Aaron" to "And the Lord spoke to Moses," increasing his importance in the incident. Verse 11 has the simple "wrath" (ὀργή), and not "*the* wrath," as in the MT (see 1.c above). Yet while the Hebrew text says that "the plague has begun," the LXX reads: "wrath...began to smite the people." It thus moves in the direction of a personification of "wrath," found in later Judaic interpretation of the verse. Finally, the MT has the niphal or passive, "was stopped," of the plague in vv 13 and 15. This is probably the divine passive here, yet it left the issue open for later Judaic interpretation in regard to the question of "by whom" the plague was stopped. In contrast, the LXX translates by κοπάζω, "to abate."[25]

These five changes over against the MT show that the LXX translator(s) were most probably already influenced by Judaic traditions which had developed in regard to this text in the synagogue or the house of study (*beth ha-midrash*), or in both.

3. Wisdom of Solomon 18:20-25

The date of the Wisdom of Solomon is disputed. C. Larcher, who has written a three-volume commentary on the work, places its third section, including chapter eighteen, "at least around the years 15-10

---

[23] Cf. Otto Eissfeldt, *The Old Testament. An Introduction* (Oxford: Blackwell, 1966) 605 and 702. The LXX text of Num 16:41-50 (Heb 17:6-15) is found in *Numeri*, ed. John Wewers (Septuaginta III, 1) 220-22.
[24] LSJ 1252, II. 2.
[25] LSJ 978.

BCE."[26] Joseph Reider considers it to be earlier than Philo of Alexandria.[27] Others consider the reign of Claudius (37-41 CE) to be the more probable dating.[28] They all agree, however, that Alexandria is the place of writing,[29] and that Num 17:6-15 lies behind the unit.

Wisd Sol 18:1-19 describes how the firstborn are destroyed by the final and worst plague for the Egyptians (Exod 11:1 – 12:32). In Exodus, God's agent of death, a plague which will be "a destroyer" (מַשְׁחִית) in 12:13 and "the destroyer" (הַמַּשְׁחִית)[30] in v 23, will strike down all the firstborn of Egypt. The LXX of Exodus also labels the latter τὸν ὀλεθρεύοντα, "the destroyer." *Targum Pseudo-Jonathan* interprets the destroyer in v 13 as "'the angel of death' (מלאך מותא), to whom is given the power 'to destroy' (למחבלא)," and in v 23 as "the destroying angel (מלאכא מחבלא)."[31] In spite of this, Wisd Sol 18:7 says "the righteous" (the Israelites) will count on deliverance.

The following unit 18:20-25 also deals with "the righteous" (v 20), yet here a plague destroys some of them. The author here retells the experience of Num 17:6-15, especially in light of Judaic tradition, in part because of the catchwords "plague" and "the destroyer."[32] The English of the NRSV reads as follows:

---

[26] Cf. his *Le Livre de la Sagesse ou La Sagesse de Salomon* (Études Bibliques, new series 5; Paris: Gabalda, 1983) 1.161. He thinks the first section was edited in 31-30 BCE, and the second in 29-25 BCE (*ibid.*). His comment on 18:20-25 is in volume 3.1025-41, from 1985. For Palestinian Judaic traditions he is completely dependent on Louis Ginzberg, *The Legends of the Jews*.
[27] Cf. his *The Book of Wisdom* (Jewish Apocryphal Literature; New York: Harper & Brothers, 1957) 14: "some time during the last pre-Christian century."
[28] Cf. David Winston, *The Wisdom of Solomon* (AB 43; New York: Doubleday, 1979) 23, followed by George Nickelsburg, *Jewish Literature Between the Bible and the Mishnah* 184.
[29] Larcher, *Le Livre* 1.138-39, also maintains this, but thinks the author came there from elsewhere.
[30] This is the hiphil part. of שחת (BDB 1008, end of 1.). Cf. also Jastrow 851: "*destroyer*, esp. *Mashḥith*, the name of a demon of destruction."
[31] Cf. Rieder 1.97-98. On the Aramaic verb חבל in the pael as equivalent to the Hebrew הִשְׁחִית , see Jastrow 420. *Neofiti 1*, MS "M" on v 13 reads: "and the destroying angel who is appointed over death will not have power to injure (you)..." (Díez-Macho 2.71 and 437). On v 23 it reads: "the destroying angel will be (not) empowered" (2.73 and 439).
[32] Cf. on this Udo Schwenk-Bressler, *Sapienta Salomonis als ein Beispiel frühjüdischer Auslegung. Die Auslegung des Buches Genesis, Exodus 1-15 und Teilen der Wüstentradition in Sap 10-19* (BEATAJ 32; Frankfurt am Main, etc.:

20) The experience of death touched also the righteous, and a plague came upon the multitude in the desert, but the wrath did not long continue.

21) For a blameless man was quick to act as their champion; he brought forward the shield of his ministry, prayer and propitiation by incense; he withstood the anger and put an end to the disaster, showing that he was Your servant.

22) He conquered the wrath not by strength of body, nor by force of arms, but by his word he subdued the avenger, appealing to the oaths and covenants given to our ancestors.

23) For when the dead had already fallen on one another in heaps, he intervened and held back the wrath, and cut off its way to the living.

24) For on his long robe the whole world was depicted, and the glories of the ancestors were engraved on the four rows of stones, and Your majesty was on the diadem upon his head.

25) To these the destroyer yielded, these he feared; for merely to test the wrath was enough.

"The wrath" (ἡ ὀργή) which "did not long continue" in v 20 refers to "*the* wrath" in MT Num 17:11, for which the LXX only has ὀργή. In v 25 it is also "*the* wrath" (τῆς ὀργῆς). That is, "the wrath" both opens and closes this unit, showing the author's literary skill. It is called ὁ θυμός, "anger" or "wrath"[33] in v 21, and ὁ χόλος, "gall," "bitter anger," "wrath"[34] in v 22. The latter verse describes this personified attribute as "the avenger," τὸν κολάζοντα, more properly "the chastiser" or "the punisher."[35] Finally, v 25 calls him "the destroyer," ὁ ὀλεθρεύων, exactly the same term employed in LXX Exod 12:23 cited above, for which *Targum Pseudo-Jonathan* has "the destroying angel," the same as "the angel of death" in v 13.

Aaron's role in subduing "the destroyer" in the incident of Num 17:6-15 is greatly emphasized here. Moses is not even alluded to once, reflecting a tendency already found in the LXX, and possibly indicative of the author's priestly origin.

Peter Lang, 1993) 283. Schwenk-Bressler correctly points out how the author reinterprets a narrative which originally dealt with rebellion and punishment into one of deliverance (282-95, esp. 284 and 294).

[33] LSJ 810, II.4.

[34] LSJ 1997. The emendation from the ὄχλος in the MSS is now accepted by all. Cf. the apparatus in Rahlf's edition of the LXX.

[35] LSJ 971,2.

The "shield of his own ministry," which Aaron brought to fight against the plague and the wrath, consisted of two things: prayer and the propitiation of incense (Wisd Sol 18:21). "Prayer" (προσευχή), also called λόγος, "word," in v 22, involves Aaron's recalling before God the oaths taken by the people to remain faithful to Him, and the various covenants made with Him. Its origin lies in the Judaic interpretation of MT Num 17:13. Verse 12 states that Aaron "put on the incense, and made atonement for the people." This is immediately followed in v 13 by: "'He stood' between the dead and the living; and the plague was stopped." "He stood" is the Hebrew וַיַּעֲמֹד. Early Judaic tradition saw in this an allusion to the עֲמִידָה, literally "standing,"[36] but also meaning the "Standing Prayer," more commonly designated the "Tefillah," a prayer of various benedictions spoken three times daily during the week and four times on the Sabbath.[37]

The second part of Aaron's "shield of his own ministry" in Wisd Sol 18:21 consists of the propitiation of "incense," θυμίαμα. This derives directly from Num 17:12, quoted above. Interestingly, in contrast to the biblical narrative, Aaron is described here as wearing the various parts of the high priestly raiment (Wisd Sol 18:24), to which the destroyer yielded, fearing them (v 25). These garments were worn by the high priest only on the Day of Atonement, when according to Lev 16:12-13 "He shall take a censer full of coals of fire from the altar before the Lord, and two handfuls of crushed sweet incense, and he shall bring it inside the curtain 13) and put the incense on the fire before the Lord...." The author of Wisd Sol 18:20-25 was not only inspired here by the similarity in imagery (censer, fire, incense, propitiation) between Num 17:6-15 and Leviticus 16, but probably also by the prayer the high priest spoke immediately after leaving the Holy of Holies in the Jerusalem Temple on the Day of Atonement.[38]

Num 17:13 states regarding Aaron: "He stood between the dead / dying and the living; and the plague was stopped." Wisd Sol 18:23 interprets this as: "For when the dead had already fallen on one another

---

[36] Jastrow 1088, II. 1). Cf. the other use of the imagery of "withstanding" in v 21 (ἀνίστημι : LSJ 140, II: *stand against*, esp. in battle, *withstand*) and "standing" in v 23 (στάς).

[37] Jastrow 1088, II. 4), who refers to the תְּפִלָּה (1686-87), and to *Soferim* 16:12, 41b (Soncino, *The Minor Tractates* 1.293).

[38] Cf. *m. Yoma* 5:1, "in the outer space he prayed a short prayer. But he did not prolong his prayer lest he put Israel in terror" (Danby 167; Albeck 2.236). Examples of this prayer are found in *b. Yoma* 53b (Soncino 251) and *y. Yoma* 5:2, 42c (Neusner 14.138).

in heaps, standing between (the) dead and the living, he restrained[39] the (personified) Wrath and clove asunder the way to the living."[40]

The haggadic embellishment "in heaps" here is σωδηρόν, just as Philo speaks of "a heap" of corpses in *Mos.* 1.100; 2.225; and *Prob.* 119. "Clove asunder" is from the verb διασχίζω, meaning "cleave asunder, sever; make a division." A διασχίς is a "division."[41] The NRSV more freely interprets the clause as: "and cut off its [wrath's] way to the living." Yet this is basically correct, for Aaron is pictured as not only restraining the Wrath in general, but also as concretely severing his way / path in regard to those who are still living. That is, Aaron erects a barrier here. This interpretation is also found in *Targum Pseudo-Jonathan*, as will be shown in section 6.4 below.

Finally, Wisd Sol 18:25 states that the Destroyer yielded to the complete high-priestly raiment of Aaron (v 24), fearing it. "For merely to test the Wrath was 'sufficient.'"[42] The latter is the adjective ἱκανός, of things "sufficient," "adequate," of persons "*sufficient*," "*competent* to do a thing."[43] Its connection here to Aaron, the Destroyer, and the dead and the living is important for the meaning of ἱκανός in 2 Cor 2:16, as will be shown in regard to rabbinic comment on Num 17:13 in section 7.5 below.

While written in Greek, Wisd Sol 18:20-25 thus also shows close involvement with the Hebrew text of Num 17:6-15. Joseph Reider has noted other Hebraisms I did not mention above, as well as a probable mistranslation.[44] For these reasons I suggest that, like the Apostle Paul, the author was bilingual and thus had access in Alexandria (or in the synagogue of the Alexandrians in Jerusalem?[45]) to Judaic comment on the Torah also in Hebrew and Aramaic.

---

[39] On ἀνακόπτω, cf. LSJ 109, III.: check, stop.
[40] I slightly modify the NRSV here.
[41] Cf. LSJ 414 for both.
[42] I slightly modify the NRSV. The Greek πεῖρα should be understood as a (negative) "trial" here (LSJ 1354: trial, attempt; see also πειράω 1355).
[43] LSJ 825, II. and I.
[44] Cf. his *The Book of Wisdom* 214 on "the four-rowed stone of engraving" in v 24, and Zeitlin's probable suggestion that Aaron in v 21 is actually not "blameless," but a man of "peace" (*shalem* instead of *shalom*), for which he is otherwise known (p. 212).
[45] Cf. the relevant sources on this cited in Str-B 2.663-64.

4. Philo of Alexandria

While Josephus omits the passage Num 17:6-15 in his *Biblical Antiquities*,[46] Philo, who was born ca. 25 BCE and died ca. 45-50 CE,[47] comments on the narrative in two different writings.

In *Her.* 196-200 (41), Philo discusses the composition of the frankincense offering (Exod 30:34-35), and how the offering of incense is connected to giving thanks to God. The catchword "incense" then leads him in 201-02 to think of Num 17:6-15 (LXX 16:41-50). He maintains that it was not Aaron himself, but "that sacred 'Word' (λόγος)" which "ran in impetuous haste 'to stand between the living and the dead,'" when "the breaking was abated" (LXX vv 47-48). The "God-beloved" protects our soul from attack and "separates and walls off the consecrated thoughts, which veritably live, from the unholy which are truly dead" (201). The consecrated were "hedged in by the mightiest of pales, fixed in the midst to repel from the better sort the onslaught and the inroads of the worse" (202).

Here as usual Philo interprets the biblical text allegorically. It is "the sacred Word" which stands between the living and the dead. If Paul was also aware of this type of interpretation of Num 17:13 (LXX 16:48) in Hellenistic Judaism, it may have influenced his terminology in 2 Cor 2:15-16. There he states: "For we are the aroma of Christ to God among those who are being saved and among those who are perishing; 16) to the one a fragrance from death to death, to the other a fragrance from life to life." Paul and his helpers seek to proclaim the Gospel of Christ throughout the world (v 14). The Apostle may have equated Christ here with the "Word," just as in John One. As such, Christ would stand between those who are being saved and those who are perishing, depending on how they respond to the message concerning him.

Secondly, "the God-beloved," synonymous with "the sacred Word," separates and divides as by a wall[48] "the consecrated thoughts, which veritably live, from the unholy which are truly dead" (201). This imagery is repeated in 202, where the consecrated are separated[49] by the

---

[46] Cf. *Ant.* 4.62-63 (4.1) and n. "a" in the LCL edition. Somewhat like the mention of "the righteous (Israelites)" in Wisd Sol 18:20, Josephus states that the perpetrators of the rebellion in Numbers 16 maintained the victims "perished for no other crime save the zeal that they had displayed for God's worship."

[47] Cf. Erwin Goodenough, *An Introduction to Philo Judaeus* (Oxford: Basil Blackwell, 1962²) 2.

[48] Cf. LSJ 415,2. on διατειχίζω.

[49] Cf. LSJ 394 on διαζεύγνυμι : part, separate.

strongest pillar[50] in the middle. It is firmly fixed,[51] repelling "from the better sort the onslaught and inroads of the worse." Here the living of Num 17:13 (LXX 16:48) are – allegorically – consecrated thoughts, and the dead the unholy (thoughts). The image of a "wall" or a "pillar" separating them was already observed in the Wisdom of Solomon above, and it will reappear in *Targum Pseudo-Jonathan*, to be analyzed in section 6. below.

In *Som.* 2.234-36 (35) Philo also deals with Num 17:6-15 (LXX 16:41-50). Directly before, in 231-33, he quotes Lev 16:17 of the high priest[52] and interprets the incense he offers as "the incense of consecrated virtues" (232). This catchword causes him to think of the incense Aaron employs in Num 17:11-12 (LXX 16:46-47), and he describes "the perfect man" in such terms. The Alexandrian philosopher maintains in 234-36 that "the man who is on the path of progress is placed by Him in the region between the living and the dead, meaning by the former those who have wisdom for their life-mate and by the latter those who rejoice in folly, 235) for we are told of Aaron that 'he stood between the dead and the living, and the breaking abated' (Num 16:48). For the man of progress does not rank either among those dead to the life of virtue, since his desires aspire to moral excellence, nor yet among those who live in supreme and perfect happiness, since he still falls short of the consummation, but is in touch with both. 236) And therefore he quite properly concludes with the phrase 'the breaking abated,' not 'ceased.'" Philo then spells out the latter.

Here the Alexandrian philosopher states allegorically that "the living" of Num 17:13 (LXX 16:48) are those who have wisdom as their life-mate, and "the dead" of the same verse are those who rejoice in folly. That is, they too are actually still alive, but choose a behavior which ultimately leads to death. As in *Her.* 201-02 above, Philo is here a witness to how the Apostle Paul – roughly his contemporary – could also employ the life and death imagery of Num 17:13 in 2 Cor 2:15-16 in a metaphorical sense.

---

[50] Cf. LSJ 1255 on ὅρος: *boundary*, landmark; 1256 – limit, fixed place; II. b. pillar; c. boundary stone.
[51] Cf. LSJ 1399, IV, on πήγνυμι.
[52] In 2.189 he had interpreted this text of the Logos. Cf. Colson and Whitaker's note "a" on 231 in the LCL edition.

5. 4 Maccabees 7:11

Fourth Maccabees was composed in Greek, most probably towards the end of Caligula's reign, i.e. ca. 40 CE, and in Antioch in Syria.[53] One of its main narratives deals in 5:1 – 7:23[54] with the torture and martyrdom by Antiochus IV Epiphanes of Eleazar, a "leader of the flock," "of priestly family, learned in the law, (and) advanced in age" (5:4). He was named (cf. 6:5 – "like a true Eleazar") after that son of Aaron who succeeded him as high priest after the father's death (Num 20:25-28 and Deut 10:6; cf. Num 17:1 and 4).

The author of Fourth Maccabees describes Eleazar's inner triumph over torture in 7:11-12: "For just as our father Aaron, armed with the censer, ran through the multitude of the people and conquered the fiery angel, 12) so the descendant of Aaron, Eleazar, though being consumed by the fire, remained unmoved in his reason."

Verse 11 clearly alludes to Num 17:6-15 *in Judaic tradition*. "The fiery angel" is the Greek τὸν ἐμπυριστὴν...ἄγγελον. The noun ὁ ἐμπυριστής means "one who sets on fire."[55] This is why "the" (τὸν) has been proposed as an emendation before ἄγγελον, as is found in some MSS.[56] Then "the one who sets on fire" would be explained by "the angel." Yet the expression is more probably an Hebraism, "the angel of fire" (מלאך השרפה or מלאך האש), lit. "angel of the fire," yet meant as "the fiery angel," as in the NRSV. While in rabbinic sources it is the angel Gabriel who consumes by fire,[57] here the reference is clearly to "the Wrath" of Num 17:11, described above in Wisd Sol 18:25 as the Destroyer (and also as such in *Targ. Ps.-Jon.* Num 17:11 – see section 6. below). "Wrath" (קֶצֶף) is also the name of one of the five angels of destruction,[58] who

---

[53] Cf. Moses Hadas, *The Third and Fourth Books of Maccabees* (Jewish Apocryphal Literature; New York: Harper & Brothers, 1953) 96 and 110-11. He is followed by Nickelsburg, *Jewish Literature* 226.
[54] Cf. the probable source of this in 2 Macc 6:18-31.
[55] LSJ 549. Both ἐμπυρίζω and ἐμπυρεύω mean to set on fire.
[56] Cf. the apparatus in Rahlf's LXX.
[57] Cf. for example *b. Pesaḥ.* 118a-b (Soncino 609), and *Pesiq. R.* 35/2 on Dan 3:25, where R. Eliezer (b. Hyrcanus, a second generation Tanna: *Introduction* 77) says the angel Gabriel "'consumed in fire' (שרף) Sennacherib's entire camp" (Friedmann 160b, Braude 673).
[58] Cf. *Exod. Rab.* Ki Thissa 41/7 on Exod 32:6 (Mirqin 6.141, Soncino 3.478-79); *Deut. Rab.* 'Eqeb 3/11 on Deut 9:1 (Mirqin 11.62, Soncino 7.78); and *Targ. Ps.-Jon.* Deut 9:19 (Rieder 2.268, Clarke 32). On the angels of destruction, see also Peter

also destroy in part through fire. "The fiery angel" thus most probably refers here to the angel "Wrath," who destroys by fire, just as God in His wrath consumed by fire Korah and his company along with Dathan and Abiram in the preceding episode in Num 16:35 and 17:4, and Aaron's sons Nadab and Abihu in the similar account of Lev 10:1-3. Elsewhere the Destroyer / the Destroying Angel is equated with the Angel of Death.[59]

6. The Targums

While the *Fragmentary Targum* is lacking for Num 17:6-15, the other targums, *Onqelos, Pseudo-Jonathan* and *Neofiti 1*, are available at this point. They reflect early and in part later Judaic interpretation of the pericope, just as the related rabbinic sources do, which will be analyzed in the next section. For our purposes, the following four are the most important haggadic embellishments of the Hebrew text.

6.1 Sweet-smelling or Aromatic Incense

In Num 17:11 Moses tells Aaron: "Take your censer, put fire on it from the altar and lay *incense* on it, and carry it quickly to the congregation and make atonement for them. For wrath has gone out from the Lord; the plague has begun." In v 12 Aaron thus "put on *the incense,* and made atonement for the people." Standing between the dead and the living, Aaron thus caused God to stop the plague (v 13).

The Hebrew of the words italicized above is קְטֹרֶת and הַקְּטֹרֶת. The usually reticent *Targum Onqelos* turns these into קטורת בוסמין and קטורת בוסמיא, respectively: "aromatic incense."[60] *Targum Pseudo-Jonathan* has קטורת בוסמין twice.[61] That is, the more expansive *Targum Pseudo-Jonathan* and the more official *Targum Onqelos* both emphasize the "aroma," "fragrance" or "sweet odor" of the incense at this point.

Schäfer, *Rivalität zwischen Engeln und Menschen. Untersuchungen zur rabbinischen Engelvorstellung* (Studia Judaica 8; Berlin: de Gruyter, 1975) 65-67.
[59] Cf. for example *Frag. Targ.* Exod 4:25-26 (Klein 1.71 and 165, and 2.36 and 124) and *Targ. Neofiti 1* on the same verses (Díez-Macho 2.25, McNamara 24).
[60] Cf. Sperber 1.252, and Grossfeld 117, who here translates "aromatic spices."
[61] Rieder 2.218. Clarke (237) translates with "aromatic incense" both times. Cf. also v 5 in both targums for the same "aromatic incense." Here Grossfeld also has this translation (p. 117).

The Hebrew בֹּשֶׂם , pl. בְּשָׂמִים , means "spice," "perfume," "sweet odor."[62] The Aramaic plural can be either בּוּסְמִין or בּוּסְמַיָּא , as found above.[63] In the targums of Num 17:11-12 it is meant as "incense with a sweet odor" or "aromatic incense."

Since Aaron is thought of as a high priest here, the expression "sweet incense" was most probably borrowed from the holiest act of the Jewish high priest, his entering the Holy of Holies in the later Jerusalem Temple and putting incense on the fire before the Lord on the annual Day of Atonement. Lev 16:12 already mentions crushed or fine "sweet incense," and *Targum Onqelos* and *Pseudo-Jonathan* again expand the simple form "incense" in v 13 twice to "incense with a sweet odor" or "aromatic incense," emphasizing the motif.[64]

Num 17:13 says Aaron "put on the incense, and made atonement for the people." On the Day of Atonement the high priest sprinkles the blood of the goat of the sin offering upon the mercy seat in the Holy of Holies, thus making "atonement for the Sanctuary because of the uncleanness of the people of Israel, and because of 'their transgressions,' all their sins" (Lev 16:16). *Targums Onqelos* and *Pseudo-Jonathan* interpret "their transgressions" here as "their rebellions" (מרדיהון).[65] The latter terminology is also substituted by them at v 21, where the high priest (Aaron) lays both hands on the scapegoat and "confesses over it all the iniquities of the people of Israel, and all 'their transgressions,' all their sins...."[66] The catchword "rebellion" certainly reminded the authors or groups of sages / scribes who composed *Targums Onqelos* and *Pseudo-Jonathan* on Numbers 17, dealing with the people's "rebellion" against Moses, of popular interpretation of Lev 16:16 and 21. The latter also deal with acts of rebellion. This aided them in transferring the motif of "incense with a sweet odor" or "aromatic incense" from Lev 16:12 and 13 to Num 17:11 and 12.

---

[62] BDB 141. The term סַם ,"*spice* used in incense," is related (BDB 702). In the plural it is usually translated in the NRSV in connection with incense as "(the) fragrant incense."

[63] Jastrow 147 on בּוּסְמָא , etc.

[64] For *Onqelos*, cf. Sperber 1.193; for *Pseudo-Jonathan*, see Rieder 2.169.

[65] Cf. Sperber 1.194 and Grossfeld 33 for *Onqelos*, and Rieder 2.169 and Maher 63 for *Pseudo-Jonathan*. The noun is מרד , מרדא (Jastrow 836): desertion, rebellion; pl. rebellious acts.

[66] Cf. Sperber 1.194 and Grossfeld 34 for *Onqelos*, and Rieder 2.170 and Maher 64 for *Pseudo-Jonathan*.

I suggest that the Apostle Paul, bilingual, was acquainted with the above terminology of incense with a "sweet odor" still found in two major targums to Num 17:11 and 12. These verses are immediately followed by imagery of the dead and the living (v 13). In a situation of individual and congregational rebellion against him, they provided Paul with the major source for both his imagery of fragrance (ὀσμή), aroma (εὐωδία), and of those being saved / remaining alive and those perishing in 2 Cor 2:14-16.[67]

6.2 The Destroyer

Targum Pseudo-Jonathan on Num 17:11 states that Aaron should place sweet-smelling incense on the fire of his censer "and carry it quickly to the congregation and make atonement for their sake, for 'the Destroyer' which had been restrained at Horeb, whose name is 'Wrath,' has come out with a mandate from before the Lord, to begin to kill." Verse 12 then has Aaron do this, "and behold, 'Wrath,' 'the Destroyer,' had begun to destroy the people."[68] Here "Wrath" is קצף as in "the Wrath" (הַקֶּצֶף) in the MT of v 11, "the Destroyer" is מחבלא , and "to destroy" is לחבלא . *Targum Neofiti 1* has here "His anger" (רוגזה),[69] and "the destruction" (חבלה) has begun "destructing" (מחבל) in v 11, and "the Destroyer" (מחבלה) had begun "destructing" (מחבל) in v 12.[70]

---

[67] Harold Attridge did not recognize the background of these "olfactory images" (ὀσμή and εὐωδία) in Judaic interpretation of Num 17:6-15. Cf. his "Making Scents of Paul. The Background and Sense of 2 Cor 2:14-17" in *Early Christianity and Classical Culture. Comparative Studies in Honor of Abraham J. Malherbe*, ed. John Fitzgerald et al. (NovTSup 110; Leiden: Brill, 2003) 71-88. Nevertheless, his characterization of ὀσμὴ ἐκ ζωῆς in 2 Cor 2:16 as "healing unguent," and ὀσμὴ ἐκ θανάτου as "embalming unguent" (applied to a corpse at death) is helpful (p. 88). M. Margareta Gruber in *Herrlichkeit in Schwachheit* 125-39 sees Exod 30:22-28, reflected in Sir 24:15, as the background of 2 Cor 2:14c-16's fragrance metaphors. She appears to have only a secondary knowledge of rabbinic sources (see for example 131, n. 143; 137 with Strack-Billerbeck; and her summary statement regarding the Old Testament – Jewish background of the fragrance metaphor on p. 138). In regard to the Apostle's use of ὀσμή , she aptly speaks of "der konkretbildhaft denkende Semit Paulus" (p. 138).
[68] Rieder 2.218; I modify the English of Clarke, 237.
[69] Jastrow 1456 on רגז , רגוז II.: anger, wrath. רוגז is the same.
[70] Cf. Díez-Macho 4.161-62 on these two verses. The marginal reading at v 11 is "the Destroyer" (מחבלנה).

From the verb חבל, חביל, the pael meaning "to injure," "to ruin," "to destroy,"[71] both מְחַבְּלָא[72] and מחבלה[73] mean "the Destroyer." They reflect a Judaic tradition already attested in Wisd Sol 18:25's ὁ ὀλεθρεύων, the same as "the Wrath," and also based on "the Wrath" in Num 17:11. These passages are especially significant for the meaning and derivation of "the Destroyer" in 1 Cor 10:10, to be analyzed in section 8. below.

6.3 Praying

Targ. Ps.-Jon. Num 17:13 says that after Aaron put sweet-smelling incense onto his censer and made atonement for the people, he "stood among them 'in prayer' and made a partition with the censer between the dead and the living; then the plague ceased."[74] The expression "in prayer" is בצלו,[75] with the noun צְלוֹ, "prayer."[76] *Targum Neofiti 1* on the same verse says Aaron "stood among the dead, 'begging mercy' for the living."[77] The Aramaic is בעי רחמין.[78] Both targums reflect early Judaic interpretation of Aaron's "standing" in the same verse, thought of as being similar to the "Standing Prayer" or *'Amidah*, as explained above in regard to the *proseuchē* of Wisd Sol 18:21.

6.4 A Partition

Targ. Ps.-Jon. Num 17:13 has Aaron not only stand among the people "in prayer." He also "made 'a partition' with the censer between the dead and the living; then the plague ceased." The term "partition" here is מְחִיצוּתָא,[79] meaning "partition," "wall," from the basic meaning of "division."[80] The Targum says "he made" (עבד)[81] this partition, with the connotation of "erecting" something like a wall. The meaning is the same as in the verb διασχίζω used of Aaron in Wisd Sol 18:23 above,

---

[71] Jastrow 420, 1). It corresponds to the Hebrew הִשְׁחִית.
[72] Jastrow 757.
[73] I consider this a variant of the latter. Cf. the term in n. 70, with a *nun*.
[74] Clarke 237.
[75] Rieder 2.218.
[76] Jastrow 1282.
[77] Translation by McNamara in Díez-Macho 4.100; the Aramaic is on p. 163.
[78] Cf. Jastrow 181 and 1468, respectively, on these words.
[79] Rieder 2.218.
[80] Jastrow 761, with the related Hebrew on p. 760.
[81] Jastrow 1035.

64   *Judaic Imagery of Rebellion*

and in several rabbinic sources, to be analyzed in the next section. Aaron's "making a partition" with his censer between the dead and the living, completely separating them, is a further haggadic embellishment of the Hebrew text.

The above four motifs emphasized in the targums, from the usually more reticent *Onqelos* to the more expansive *Pseudo-Jonathan* and *Neofiti 1*, are also reflected in rabbinic sources, to which they are closely related and to which I now turn.

7. Rabbinic Sources

A number of motifs and even exact terminology similar to that in 2 Cor 2:14-17 are found in rabbinic writings.

7.1 The Angel of Death

As pointed out in section 3. above, "the Destroyer" can also be labeled "the Angel of Death" (מלאך המות).[82] The latter is especially true for the interpretation of Num 17:12-13 in the incident of Moses' receiving the Torah in heaven from God, against the great objections of the ministering angels. In *b. Šabb.* 88b-89a, for example, R. Joshua b. Levi, a first generation Palestinian Amora,[83] relates the following:

> When Moses ascended on high, the ministering angels spoke before the Holy One, blessed be He: "Sovereign of the Universe! What business has one born of woman among us?" "He has come to receive the Torah," He answered them. They said to Him: "That secret treasure which has been hidden by You for nine hundred and seventy-four generations before the world was created You desire to give to flesh and blood?" (Then they denigrate Moses by citing Ps 8:5 [Eng. 4] with "What is 'man'?" God thereupon tells Moses to give the angels an answer, so he cites several of the Ten Commandments from Exod 20:2-15. The ministering angels concede that these do not apply to them, but rather to humans, and they thus decide to present Moses with gifts.) Immediately each was moved to love [Moses] and transmitted something to him, as it is said: "You have ascended on high, you have taken spoils [the Torah]; you have received *gifts* on

---

[82] Cf. the Angel of Death as also equivalent to "the Wrath" of Num 17:11 in *Num. Rab.* Bemidbar 5/7 on Num 4:19 (Mirqin 9.105, Soncino 5.151).
[83] *Introduction* 92.

account of *man*" (Ps 68:19, Eng. 18). "As a recompense for their calling you 'man,' you received 'gifts.'" The Angel of Death also gave him something, for it is said: "He put on the incense, and made atonement for the people" (Num 17:12). And it is said: "He stood between the dead and the living," etc. (v 13). If he had not told this to [Moses], how would he have known it?[84]

The above tradition is found in many variations in various sources, showing its great popularity.[85] One of them is the late *Midrash ha-Gadol* on Exod 19:20. It notes that the ministering angels at the close of the debate gave Moses "a multitude of secrets." Noticing this, the Angel of Death also revealed a "secret" (מסתירין)[86] to him, the use of incense in Num 17:11-13.[87]

Midr. Pss. 68/11 on Ps 68:19 interprets the words of this verse, "those who 'rebel' against the Lord God's abiding there," as applying to the Israelites "who had also been rebellious, but among whom the presence of God came to dwell after they accepted the Torah."[88] The motif of "rebelliousness" may have helped to associate this Psalm verse with the rebellion described in Num 17:6-15, especially in Judaic sources.

Finally, the oldest Judaic chronology, *Seder 'Olam*, states in 6 that Moses "descended (with the Torah on the second set of tablets) on the 10th of Tishre, that is, Yom Kippur."[89] This is also found in *Pirq. R. El.* 46

---

[84] I slightly modify the translation of I. Epstein in Soncino 421-23; see especially his n. 2 on p. 423.

[85] Cf. for example *Pesiq. R.* 20/4 (Friedmann 98a, Braude 409-10) and the other sources cited in Str-B 3.596-98; Schäfer, *Rivalität* 128-31; and David Halpern, *The Faces of the Chariot. Early Jewish Responses to Ezekiel's Vision* (TSAJ 16; Tübingen: Mohr Siebeck, 1988) 301-05. See also Rashi on Num 17:11 (pp. 84-85). As noted in section I. 11. 9, I see no convincing evidence that merkabah mysticism, connected to Psalm 68, is present in 2 Cor 2:14. On this assertion, see James Scott, "The Triumph of God in 2 Cor 2.14: Additional Evidence of Merkabah Mysticism in Paul" in *NTS* 42 (1996) 260-81, heavily dependent on Halperin at this point. Scott's passing reference to Num 17:13 is prefaced by a "perhaps" (p. 274).

[86] Jastrow 806: the plural of the Greek loanword μυστήριον is meant as the singular here.

[87] Cf. Kook 2.395-96. The "secret" of Soncino 423 on *b. Šabb.* 89a is not in the text ("a thing," "something"), but is meant so because it was hidden before. See also the Torah as "that secret treasure" in 88b (Soncino 421).

[88] Buber 319, Braude 1.546. Cf. also the interpretation of this verse in *Cant. Rab.* 6:5 § 1 (Soncino 9.263).

[89] Guggenheimer 74-75.

in the name of Ben Bethera just after the interpretation of Ps 68:19 as gifts given to Moses by the angels.[90] The association of Moses' ascent to heaven to receive the Torah, the Angel of Death and Ps 68:19, and Moses' following descent on the Day of Atonement may also have aided in associating imagery of the high priest with the description of Aaron in Num 17:12-13, for example in Wisd Sol 18:21 and 24.

In spite of the latter, it is important to note that the Judaic tradition of Moses' ascent to heaven and his encounter with the Angel of Death, related to Num 17:6-15, emphasizes not Aaron's but *Moses'* role. It is he, not Aaron, to whom this secret, the salvific use of incense, is revealed. Aaron only receives it second-hand from Moses. This is significant for Paul's use of "sweet-smelling fragrance" in the unit 2 Cor 2:14-17 (see section 6. below).

7.2 Prayer

Deut 32:36 states of God: "Indeed the Lord will vindicate His people, have compassion on His servants, when He sees that their power is gone, neither bond nor free remaining." *Sifre* Ha'azinu 326 on this verse comments: "When He sees that there are no men among them who would 'plead for mercy' for them, as did Aaron, as it is said: 'He stood between the dead and the living; and the plague was stopped' (Num 17:13)."[91]

The expression "plead for mercy" here is מבקשים ... רחמים . *Midrash ha-Gadol* on Deut 32:36's "when He sees that their power is gone" comments: "For they have no one like Aaron who will stand and 'pray' for them, as it is said: 'And he stood between the dead and the living' (Num 17:13)."[92]

The *Sifre* passage is definitely Tannaitic and corroborates the early dating of Wisd Sol 18:21-22 with Aaron's "prayer" and his "word" in connection with Num 17:11-13, and both *Targum Pseudo-Jonathan* and *Targum Neofiti 1* on Num 17:13. The latter has "begging for mercy" as in *Sifre*, and the former "in prayer," as in the late midrash collection *Midrash ha-Gadol*, which at times has preserved very early traditions.

---

[90] Eshkol 179; Friedlander 362 with n. 8. On a possible identification of this rabbi, cf. *Introduction* 83 regarding the second generation Tanna Yehudah ben Bathyra / Betera.
[91] Finkelstein 378, Hammer 339.
[92] Kook 5.727.

7.3 The Dead and the Living

Tanḥ. Teṣaweh 15 comments on Exod 30:1, "You shall make an altar on which to offer incense." Among other things it relates the following. "See how beloved incense is through the fact that the plague was halted by incense, as Moses said to Aaron: (Num 17:11-12). What is meant by 'the plague has begun' (v 11)?" R. Judah b. Simon (a fourth generation Palestinian Amora)[93] stated: "The Angel (of Death) administered the doses of poison in sequence, neglecting neither the dead among the living nor the living among the dead. That is, he administered them in rotation, as it is said: 'the plague had already begun among the people' (v 12). As it is also said: 'begin to count...from the time the sickle is first put to the standing grain' (Deut 16:9). Just as one reaps row by row, so the plague acted upon the people (in rotation): Num 17:12."

The midrash continues by stating that Aaron found the Angel (of Death) standing and injuring / destroying the people. Aaron thus stood before him and would not permit him to continue injuring / destroying. Yet "he (the Angel of Death) stood among the dead" (v 13) and told Aaron to let him go in order that he could carry out his commission. Aaron then argues that the Angel of Death's commission may be from God, yet Moses commissioned him, Aaron. The only way to resolve the issue is for both to go to the tent of meeting, where both Moses and God are. When the Angel refused, Aaron "seized him by the loins and dragged him in, as it is said: 'Aaron returned to Moses at the entrance of the tent of meeting, and the plague was stopped' (v 15)."[94] Here God is pictured as decreeing the superiority of Moses over the Angel of Death at the tent of meeting, and the preliminary ceasing of the plague in v 13 is made complete in v 15.

It is very important to note the metaphorical language here. The Angel of Death neglects "neither the dead among the living nor the living among the dead." While this imagery derives from a fourth century Amora, it shows how the Apostle Paul at an earlier point, but standing in the same Judaic tradition, could similarly employ the terms "the dead and the living" from Num 17:13 in a metaphorical sense in 2 Cor 2:15-16. He and his co-workers in the Gospel now stand between those who are being saved and those who are perishing. The former are

---

[93] *Introduction* 103.
[94] Eshkol 389; Berman 563-64, whom I slightly modify. Rashi quotes this midrash in his comment on Num 17:11-15 (Rosenbaum and Silberbaum 84, with n. 1).

a fragrance from death to death for some, and for others from life to life.[95]

7.4 Salvation

Num. Rab. Bemidbar 4/20 on Num 4:16 states:

> Our Rabbis said: "There were two things which were really holy and great but which men wrongly considered to be dangerous, and in order that a stigma should not be attached to them, a striking instance of their praiseworthiness and 'blessedness' has been recorded. These are the things: The incense and the ark. 'The incense': That men might not say the incense was dangerous, having been the cause of the death of Nadab and Abihu (Lev 10:1-2) and the cause through which the congregation of Korah was burned (Num 15:35) as well as the medium through which Uzziah was stricken with leprosy (2 Chron 26:19), the Holy One, blessed be He, recorded the great distinction of the incense in that it was the instrument whereby Israel 'was delivered'; as it says: 'So Aaron took it as Moses had ordered, and ran into the middle of the assembly, where the plague had already begun among the people. He put on the incense,' etc., 'and the plague was stopped' (Num 17:12-13). ... All this is to teach you that it is not the incense and the ark that kill, but sins that kill."[96]

The Hebrew verb in "Israel 'was delivered'" is וְנִצְּלוּ ,"they were saved."[97] It is important to note that it is the (sweet-smelling odor of the) incense in Num 17:12-13 which leads to the Israelites' being saved, terminology very similar to 2 Cor 2:15, "For we are the aroma of Christ to God among 'those who are saved (τοῖς σῳζομένοις)'...."

---

[95] This proposal helps to explain "one of the more puzzling aspects of Paul's metaphorical utterance, and that is the yoking together of the fragrance imagery with the stark dualistic contrast between those being saved and those perishing, between death and life" (Regina Plunkett-Dowling, *Reading and Restoration* 45-46). My suggestion also shows that other rabbinic passages on the Torah as an odor of (leading to) life or death are of no direct relevance here. Cf. Jacobus Wettstein, *Novum Testamentum Graecum*, Tomus II (Amsterdam: Dommerian, 1752; reprint Graz: Akademische Druck- und Verlagsanstalt, 1962) 182, and Str-B 3.498-99. T. W. Manson employs them in "2 Corinthians 2 14-17 : Suggestions towards an exegesis" in *Studia Paulina* 155-62.

[96] Mirqin 9.91; Soncino 5.129-30, which I modify.

[97] Cf. the niphal of נצל in Jastrow 929: to be rescued, saved.

The salvific effect of incense as described in the above midrash is labeled a "blessing" (בְּרָכָה) , translated "blessedness" above. This basic tradition is definitely Tannaitic, as shown in Mek. Vayassaʿ 7 on Exod 17:5[98] and Mek. R. Šim. b. Yoḥ. Beshallaḥ on the same verse, although they apply "blessing" here to the ark.[99]

Another rabbinic tradition also speaks of "saving" in the same context as above. Tanḥ. B Ṣaw 12 on Lev 8:2, "Take Aaron and his sons," relates the following:

> Why is "take" mentioned here? The Holy One, blessed be He, said to Moses: "I am duty-bound to taking. Rise and magnify him (Aaron) through taking." And when did he (Moses) take Aaron? At the time "the Wrath went forth" (Num 17:11) upon those who hate Israel. Moses said to him: "Take your censer, put fire upon it (from the altar and lay incense upon it..." –ibid.).[100] (Because of the incident of his sons' death in Lev 10:1-2, Aaron now fears his own death if he carries out Moses' command.) Moses said to him: "Go and act quickly; for as you are talking, they are dying. Only 'go quickly to the congregation and make atonement for them' (Num 17:11)." When Aaron heard that, he said: "If I die for Israel, am I not adequate?" Immediately "Aaron took it as Moses had ordered" (v 12). Therefore the Holy One, blessed be He, said to Moses: "Take Aaron..." (Lev 8:2). He magnified him through taking. "Just as Aaron (in the future) is going 'to save' his children (the Israelites in Num 17:12-13) by taking, so you are to magnify him through taking." Thus it is said: "Take Aaron...."[101]

The Hebrew of "to save" here is לְהַצִּיל . Acting on orders from Moses, his brother in the future (for Numbers is after Leviticus) will "save" the Israelites from the Wrath of the plague in Num 17:11-13. The parallel tradition in Tanḥ. Ṣaw 9 on Lev 8:2 has הִצִּיל , "he saved."[102] These Tanḥuma traditions show that the motif of "being saved" as found in the Numbers Rabbah incident analyzed above was not singular. It

---

[98] Lauterbach 2.131-32.
[99] Cf. Epstein and Melamed 118 on the latter. See also Tanḥ. Beshallaḥ 21 on Exod 16:33 (Eshkol 1.301, Berman 440-41).
[100] The original hearers of this narrative knew the Bible (almost) by heart and would also have had the rest of the text in mind.
[101] Buber 19; I slightly modify Townsend's translation on p. 215.
[102] Eshkol 500. It should also be noted that in Ant. 4,12 in regard to the entire episode of Korah's rebellion, Josephus states that Moses "saved" (ἔσωσε) the Israelites from the peril of destruction there.

belonged to basic Judaic interpretation of Num 17:11-13, from which the Apostle Paul borrowed it in 2 Cor 2:15. Paul and his fellow missionaries, like Aaron and his incense, "are the aroma of Christ 'among those who are being saved (ἐν τοῖς σῳζομένοις)'...."

7.5 Sufficient

In *Tanḥ*. B Ṣaw 12 on Lev 8:2, cited in the previous section, Num 17:11 is quoted, followed by: "When Aaron heard that, he said: 'If I die for Israel, am I not *adequate* ?' Immediately 'Aaron took it as Moses had ordered' (v 12)." The midrash then continues with Aaron's "saving" the Israelites through the actions performed in vv 12-13, which include the use of incense.[103]

The italicized word "adequate" above is the Hebrew כְּדַיִי , for which the parallel tradition in *Tanḥ*. Ṣaw 9 on the same verse has the minor variant כְּדַאי.[104] This adjective, which derives from the noun דַי , "sufficiency," "being enough,"[105] means "adequate," "worthy," "competent," "deserving," "sufficient."[106] Here the appropriate translation is "adequate," as Townsend has, or "sufficient." Aaron asks his brother Moses whether his death would not be sufficient if he put incense on the censer in order to stop the Wrath, that is, the plague (Num 17:11). In light of the deaths of his two sons Nadab and Abihu through the improper application of incense (Lev 10:1-3), this was a justified fear. Nevertheless, he immediately did as Moses had ordered him (Num 17:12). It also may be implied here that Aaron hoped his death alone, without any further deaths, would be sufficient to stop the Wrath, the death-bringing plague.

I suggest that the Apostle Paul was aware of this haggadic interpretation of Num 17:11-13 in an earlier form and borrowed not only the term "saving" from it, but also the term "sufficient." In 2 Cor 2:16 he asks after mentioning the saved, the dying, death and life: "Who is 'sufficient' for these things?" The Greek of "sufficient" is ἱκανός, meaning of persons "sufficient," "competent to do" a thing.[107]

---

[103] Buber 19, Townsend 215.
[104] Eshkol 500.
[105] Jastrow 293. Cf. also BDB 191: "sufficiency," "enough."
[106] Jastrow 613. See also the noun with these forms, meaning "sufficiency," "worthiness," on p. 614.
[107] LSJ 825, I.; BAGD 374: "sufficient," "adequate." The latter classify 2 Cor 2:16 in "2. fit, appropriate, competent, qualified, able, with the connotation worthy." Yet here, as in the NRSV, the basic meaning is "sufficient." In 3:5-6 it is rather

Judaic Imagery of Rebellion

The commentators have had a major problem with the meaning of this question in its context. Alfred Plummer sees Paul "flashing out this question in a way which...is almost offensive, and is certainly abrupt."[108] R. H. Strachan notes that the connection between it "and verse 17 is not quite obvious."[109] For this reason Hans Windisch presumed "the poorly made transition" pointed to some intervening words having dropped out, or to a pause in dictation.[110] Jan Lamprecht considers 2:16b to be "properly a question of resignation. The implied answer is: Of course, nobody is adequate from and by him- or herself (cf. 3:5). This appears to be Paul's first reaction."[111] Others think that while Paul does not directly answer the question, he implies the answer of "We are: I and my fellow workers in the Gospel."[112] Hans Windisch also maintains that Paul's question strongly recalls Joel 2:11, καὶ τίς ἔσται ἱκανὸς αὐτῇ, that is, who will be sufficient for the great Day of the Lord.[113] Ernest-Bernard Allo follows this suggestion, adding that Paul here feels he is before the judgment of God, yet with the "terrible sentiment of himself being its agent. This fine passage ends in a chilliness."[114] Dieter Georgi thinks the catchword "sufficiency / adequacy" derives from Paul's opponents, and the Apostle takes it up here, further developing it in 3:5-6.[115] Margaret Thrall asks whether Paul's use of ἱκανός may not derive from the call of Moses in LXX Exod 4:10, intending "an implicit contrast between Moses' self-acknowledged lack of adequacy and his own endowment with it."[116]

"competent." The LXX translates דַּי by ἱκανός at least twelve times. See Hatch-Redpath 683. In 2:14 the Greek term has nothing to do with God as שַׁדַּי. On this designation, see Karl Heinrich Rengstorf, art. ἱκανός, etc. in *TDNT* 3.294, with n. 3.

[108] Cf. his *Second Epistle of Saint Paul to the Corinthians* 72. See also Hans Lietzmann's term "ruckartig" in his *An die Korinther I-II*, 109.

[109] Cf. his *The Second Epistle of Paul to the Corinthians* 78.

[110] Cf. his *Der zweite Korintherbrief* 100. He also thinks 2:16b would better be followed by 4:6ff.

[111] Cf. his *Second Corinthians* (Sacra Pagina 8; Collegeville, MN: The Liturgical Press, 1999) 40.

[112] Cf. for example Alfred Plummer, *Second Epistle of St Paul to the Corinthians* 72, and Paul Barnett, *The Second Epistle to the Corinthians* 155.

[113] Cf. his *Der zweite Korintherbrief* 100.

[114] Cf. his *Seconde Épître aux Corinthiens* (EB; Paris: Gabalda, 1956²) 47.

[115] Cf. his *The Opponents* 233. He is followed here by Collange, *Énigmes* 37.

[116] Cf. her *The Second Epistle to the Corinthians*, Vol. I, p. 210. She cites P. R. Jones, *The Apostle Paul: A Second Moses According to II Corinthians 2:14 - 4:7* (1973 Princeton dissertation) 40 for this suggestion. See her 208-10 for a general survey of opinions on the meaning of Paul's question.

The latter is not the case, for the Apostle derived the term ἱκανός from the כדיי of Judaic interpretation of Num 17:11-12, as in the *Tanḥuma* passages cited above. Although it is Aaron who there also poses a question with the term,[117] just as Paul does in 2 Cor 2:16, he does so as a reaction to Moses' command, and after posing it, he carries out Moses' order. That is, by echoing Judaic tradition on Num 17:11-12 here, the Apostle may indeed be comparing himself with Moses. Aaron in the above haggadah got his "commission" from Moses, (but Moses his from God).[118] "In regard to these things (just mentioned in 2 Cor 2:14-16a), who is 'sufficient'?" asks Paul. The unexpressed but implied answer is indeed: "I (and my fellow workers in the Gospel)." While they are not competent / sufficient by themselves, they are as "ministers of a new covenant" (3:5-6), which is superior to the ministry of "death" and "condemnation" (vv 7 and 9) mediated by Moses at Sinai (3:7-18, in which Moses is specifically mentioned in vv 7, 13 and 15). By borrowing the term "sufficient" from Judaic interpretation of Num 17:11-12, the Apostle (or "Commissioned One") appears to have already implied his own superiority to Moses in 2 Cor 2:16b. Paul's "spreading the Gospel in every place" (with the help of his co-workers) now in the final days leads both to being saved and perishing, to life and death. This is the "horrifying truth" of vv 14-16.[119]

7.6 Fragrance and Sweet-smelling Odor

In section 6.1 above I pointed out that the Judaic traditions still reflected in *Targums Onqelos* and *Pseudo-Jonathan* on the "sweet-smelling" incense of Num 17:11-12 provided the Apostle Paul with the major

---

[117] Cf. again the connection of ἱκανός with the effect of Aaron's high-priestly raiment in Wisd Sol 18:25, dependent on Numbers 17. See also the motif of "sufficiency" at the beginning of Numbers 16 in vv 3 and 7. The latter's רב־לכם is translated in the LXX by ἱκανούσθω ὑμῖν, and the targums employ the verb סגי both times here, which can mean "to be sufficient" (Jastrow 953-54,2). See on this also *Num. Rab.* Korach 18/18 on Num 16:7 with Deut 3:26 (Mirqin 10.205; Soncino 6.729), and *b. Soṭ.* 13b (Soncino 70).

[118] Cf. the fact that Aaron must drag the Angel of Death to Moses and God at the tent of meeting for a decision in *Tanḥ.* Teṣaweh 15 on Exod 30:1 (Eshkol 389, Berman 563). There is a wordplay here with שָׁלַח, "to send," "to commission" (Jastrow 1580), and שְׁלִיחוּת, a "commission" (Jastrow 1583,2). An "apostle" is a שָׁלִיחַ (*ibid.*), one sent or commissioned.

[119] Cf. this expression in C. K. Barrett, *The Second Epistle to the Corinthians* 102 and his argumentation there.

source for his imagery of "sweet-smelling" / "fragrant" and "aromatic" in 2 Cor 2:15-16, ὀσμή [120] and εὐωδία.[121] Here I merely wish to make several supplementary remarks in regard to other Judaic traditions connected to Num 17:11-13.

Josephus in *Ant.* 8.101-02 notes that so great a quantity of incense was burned at the dedication of Solomon's Temple in Jerusalem "that all the air around was filled with it and carried its 'sweetness' to those who were at a very great distance...."[122] The adjective translated by Thackeray and Marcus as "sweetness" here is ἡδύς, "*pleasant*...to the smell," from the root ἡδύ - "sweet."[123]

Pesiq. R. 20/3 comments on Cant 5:13, interpreted as "His lips are lilies, dropping with myrrh that passes away." It notes that "when Solomon built the Temple, the whole world was filled with the 'fragrance / odor of spices / perfumes.'"[124] The first term here is רֵיחַ, "flavor," "scent," "odor."[125] It is almost always translated in the LXX by ὀσμή,[126] as found in 2 Cor 2:14 and 16. The second term is בְּשָׂמִים, the plural of בֹּשֶׂם, "spice," "perfume."[127] It is important to note that right

---

[120] LSJ 1261: "smell," "odor," in the positive sense as "fragrant odor"; BAGD 586: "fragrance," "odor," here fragrance; and the art. ὀσμή by Gerhard Delling in *TDNT* 5.493-95.

[121] LSJ 740: "sweet smell," with the verb εὐωδέω as "to be fragrant" and the adjective εὐωδής as "sweet-smelling," "fragrant"; BAGD 329 as "aroma," "fragrance"; and the art. εὐωδία by Albrecht Stumpff in *TDNT* 2.808-10. A basic study for both terms is still Ernst Lohmeyer, *Vom göttlichen Geruch* (Sitzungsberichte der Heidelberger Akademie der Wissenschaften, Philosophisch-historische Klasse (Heidelberg: Carl Winter, 1919). See also Bernhard Kötting, "Wohlgeruch der Heiligkeit" in *Jenseitsvorstellungen in Antike und Christentum* (JAC Suppl. 9, Memorial Volume to Alfred Stuiber; Münster: Aschendorff, 1982) 168-75.

[122] I have added "very" to Thackeray and Marcus' "great distance" to better express the superlative πορρωτάτω. Cf. LSJ 1533, II., on προσωτέρω : furthest distant.

[123] LSJ 765. Cf. 2 Chron 2:3 (Eng. 4), where Solomon tells Hiram he is about to dedicate the Temple to God "for offering 'fragrant incense' before Him." The latter is קְטֹרֶת־סַמִּים in the MT, but "incense, a compound" in the LXX.

[124] Friedmann 96b; Braude 404 translates freely.

[125] Jastrow 1474; BDB 926: scent, odor, also of ointments.

[126] Cf. Hatch-Redpath 1018-19.

[127] Jastrow 199, BDB 141-42. Cf. the pl. בשמים as "spice," "perfume," "sweet odor" in BDB 141, and בָּסֵם, בָּשֵׂם in Jastrow 179 as "to be sweet."

afterwards, *Pesiq. R.* 20/4[128] records the haggadah analyzed above of the Angel of Death's giving a present to Moses, together with Ps 68:19 and the incense of Num 17:11-13.[129] In *b. Šabb.* 88b R. Joshua b. Levi also comments on Cant 5:13, stating: "With every single word that went forth from the mouth of the Holy One, blessed be He, the whole world was filled with spices / fragrance."[130] He then relates the same haggadah as in *Pesiq. R.* 20/4 with the same biblical references.[131]

It thus seems quite probable that the phrase "the whole world was filled with the odor / fragrance of (sweet-smelling) spices / perfumes" was also at an earlier stage connected to Judaic interpretation of Num 17:11-13. It is from this larger context that the Apostle Paul may have borrowed the thought of "the whole world" when in 2 Cor 2:14 he maintains: God in Christ through us spreads "in every place" (ἐν παντὶ τόπῳ) the fragrance (ὀσμή) that comes from knowing him.

8. 1 Corinthians 10:10

In 10:5 Paul maintains that God was not pleased with the majority of the Israelites in the wilderness, therefore they were "struck down" there. In v 6 the Apostle says "these things occurred as examples for us, so that we might not desire evil as they did." In v 7 he alludes to the idolaters and sexual immorality connected in Judaic tradition with the sin of the Golden Calf, and cites Exod 32:6.[132] In v 8 he expressly mentions sexual immorality, leading to the death of 23,000 in a single day. This is a clear allusion to Num 25:1-9, dealing with idolatry and the Israelite men having intercourse with the (pagan) women of Moab. After Phinehas, Aaron's grandson, zealously kills an Israelite and his female partner,[133] "the plague was stopped" (v 8), the exact terminology (וַתֵּעָצַר הַמַּגֵּפָה)

---

[128] This is a later, artificial division. Originally both 3 and 4 were simply part of parasha 20, separated for example by "another interpretation." Cf. the Friedmann text.
[129] Friedmann 98a, Braude 409-10.
[130] Soncino 421.
[131] Soncino 421-23, including 89a.
[132] On the entire section of 10:1-22, see also Wayne Meeks, "'And Rose Up to Play.' Midrash and Parenesis in 1 Corinthians 10:1-22," in *JSNT* 16 (1982) 64-78. He maintains vv 1-13 are a homily taken over and adapted by Paul. At least in regard to v 10 I consider this improbable.
[133] For the development of this zealotic motif in Judaic tradition and its relevance to John 7:53 - 8:11, see my "*Caught in the Act*," *Walking on the Sea, and the Release of Barabbas Revisited* (SFSHJ 157; Atlanta: Scholars Press, 1998) 1-48.

of Num 17:13.[134] In 25:9 the number 24,000 is given, for which Paul in 1 Cor 10:8 has the variant 23,000.[135]

The Apostle follows this in 10:9 with a reference to those who put Christ in the wilderness to the test "and were destroyed by serpents." This is a clear allusion to the incident of the Israelites' complaining ("speaking against") God and Moses in Num 21:5. Therefore the Lord sent poisonous / fiery serpents among them, which bit the people, "so that many Israelites died" (v 6).[136]

Because of the latter two references to Number 25 and 21, it is very probable that Paul's next and final example also derives from a nearby section of that biblical book. In 10:10 the Apostle writes: "And do not complain as some of them complained, and were destroyed by the Destroyer." This twofold "complaining" is an echo of Num 17:6-15 in Judaic tradition, as has been recognized by numerous scholars.[137]

The term "complain" in 1 Cor 10:10 is γογγύζω. It is the very same verb employed in the LXX at the beginning of the incident of Num 17:6-15, translating the verb לון of the MT: "The Israelites 'murmured /

---

[134] The LXX employs different nouns and verbs here.
[135] Is this a lapse of memory on the part of the Apostle? Interestingly, Josephus also has a different number (14,000) at this point in his *Ant*. 4.155. For each tribe at the time of Korah's rebellion in Numbers 16 as "represented by twenty-three men," cf. the very late source noted by Ginzberg, *Legends* 6.100.
[136] While the MT has רָב, "many," two targums increase this to "a great multitude." Cf. *Pseudo-Jonathan* (Rieder 2.224, and Clarke 247) and *Neofiti 1*, MS "M" (Díez-Macho 4.193 and 579). The incident of the bronze serpent is also alluded to in John 3:14.
[137] Cf. Heinrich Meyer, *Erster Brief an die Korinther* (Meyer; Göttingen: Vandenhoeck & Ruprecht, 1849²) 207; Johannes Weiss, *Der erste Korintherbrief* (Meyer; Göttingen: Vandenhoeck & Ruprecht, 1910) 253; Archibald Robertson and Alfred Plummer, *The First Epistle of Saint Paul to the Corinthians* (ICC; Edinburgh: Clark, 1958²) 206; Christian Wolff, *Der erste Brief an die Korinther* (THNT 7/2; Berlin: Evangelische Verlagsanstalt, 1982²) 45; Friedrich Lang, *Die Briefe an die Korinther* (NTD 7; Göttingen: Vandenhoeck & Ruprecht, 1986) 126; Christophe Senft, *La première Épître de Saint Paul aux Corinthiens* (CNT 7; Geneva: Labor et Fides, 1990) 130-31; and Jacob Kremer, *Der erste Brief an die Korinther* (RNT; Regensburg: Friedrich Pustet, 1997) 206. Robertson and Plummer (206) correctly state in regard to the alternative reference often suggested by others: "The murmuring against the report of the spies can hardly be meant, for that was punished by the murmurers dying off in the wilderness, not by any special destruction (Num. xiv. 1,2,29)."

complained' the next day regarding Moses and Aaron, saying..."(v 6).[138] As I pointed out in the introduction to section II., the extant targums render the Hebrew verb here by "rebelling." The same Greek verb γογγύζω is used in LXX Num 17:20, and the noun γογγυσμός occurs in vv 20 and 25. Because of all this "murmuring / complaining" in 17:6, 20 and 25, Tannaitic Judaic tradition in *Mek. R. Ish.* Vayassaʿ 7 on Exod 17:5 maintains that there were "three things about which the Israelites used to 'complain' and say that they were sorts of punishment. These three were: The incense, the ark, and the rod. They used to say: This incense is but a means of punishment. It was this that killed Nadab and Abihu. For it is said: 'And Nadab and Abihu the sons of Aaron took,' etc. (Lev 10:1). Therefore the people should know that it was really a means of atonement, as it is said: 'And he put on incense, and made atonement for the people' (Num 17:12)." After a discussion of the ark, the "rod" is mentioned, which is (referred to also in 17:16-26, connected to "complaints" in vv 20 and 25, and is) actually "a means of performing miracles."[139]

If Paul was aware of the above haggadic tradition in an earlier form, its motif of "complaining" may also have helped him to think of Num 17:6 (to 15) as the background for his imagery of "complaining" in 1 Cor 10:10. This is corroborated by the next half of the Apostle's statement.

Paul asserts that the complainers "were destroyed by the Destroyer." This NRSV translation (without capitalization) implies a wordplay in the Greek, which is not the case. The Greek of "were destroyed" is ἀπώλοντο, from ἀπόλλυμι, "destroy utterly," "kill."[140] It alludes here to those killed by the plague (14,700) in Num 17:13-14.

"The Destroyer" in 1 Cor 10:10 is ὁ ὀλοθρευτής, which only occurs here in the NT and the LXX.[141] As pointed out in section 6.2 above, Paul borrows it from Judaic interpretation of Num 17:11-12. There *Targum Pseudo-Jonathan*, for example, has Moses tell Aaron in v 11 to place sweet-smelling incense on the fire of his censer "and carry it quickly to the congregation and make atonement for their sake, for 'the Destroyer'

---

[138] Both the Hebrew New Testaments of Delitzsch (p. 316) and the United Bible Societies (p. 432) also employ the verb לוּן for γογγύζω here.

[139] Cf. Lauterbach 2.131-32 with תַּרְעוֹמֶת, "murmur, complaint, quarrel" (Jastrow 1701), and the verb רָעַם, to be rebellious, to murmur (1487). Exod 17:3 has the people "murmur / complain" against Moses.

[140] LSJ 207; BAGD 95: "ruin," "destroy."

[141] LSJ 1217 can only cite this passage. Cf. also BAGD 564; the art. ὀλοθρευτής by Johannes Schneider in *TDNT* 5.169-70; and Str-B 3.412-16.

(מְחַבְּלָא) which had been restrained at Horeb, whose name is 'Wrath' (קֶצֶף), has come out with a mandate from before the Lord, to begin to kill." Verse 12 has Aaron do this, "and behold, 'Wrath,' 'the Destroyer,' had begun to destroy the people."[142]

Here the emphasized term "*the* Wrath" of MT Num 17:11 (הַקֶּצֶף) receives the additional name of "the Destroyer," repeated in v 12. It had been restrained at Horeb / Sinai, when Moses ascended on high to receive the Ten Commandments (and the terrible incident of the Golden Calf occurred below). There the angels first plead with God not to allow a mortal to receive the Torah. When Moses convinces them otherwise, they all make him a gift, including the Angel of Death's revealing to him how the sweet-smelling incense of Num 17:11-12 can stop the plague, i.e. death (cf. section 7.1 above). Here the Angel of Death is equivalent to "the Destroyer," as had been surmised over 150 years ago.[143]

The above is corroborated by Wisd Sol 18:20-25, where in v 25 "the Destroyer" (ὁ ὀλεθρεύων), associated with "the Wrath" (ἡ ὀργή), is described as yielding to the full high-priestly raiment of Aaron, as well as to his use (v 21) of the incense of Num 17:11-12.[144]

In light of the above it now seems certain that Paul alludes to or "echoes" the incident of Num 17:6-15 in 1 Cor 10:10, as the commentators cited at the beginning of this section also proposed earlier. It is the last of three episodes referred to by the Apostle from the biblical book of Numbers which are "to serve as an example," "written down to instruct us, on whom the ends of the ages have come" (v 11). The Corinthians should therefore watch out that they not (similarly) fall (v 12). God, however, will provide a way out if they are also "tested" (v 13).

Paul was thus definitely aware of early Judaic tradition on Num 17:6-15. Since he already alludes to or echoes it in his own first letter to the Corinthians (10:10), this makes it all the more probable that he had precisely this passage in mind when in his second epistle to them he employs imagery from the same incident in 2:14-16.

---

[142] Cf. the references cited in the notes to section 6.2 above, including *Targum Neofiti 1* ad loc.

[143] Cf. Heinrich Meyer, *Erster Brief an die Korinther* (1849²) 207, who thought that the Angel of Death in rabbinic sources developed out of the Destroyer. He refers to Num 17:6-15.

[144] A number of commentators call attention to this passage, yet do not recognize its relevance to 1 Cor 10:10 precisely via Judaic tradition on Num 17:6-15. Heb 11:28 has the variant ὁ ὀλοθρεύων , but this refers to the destroyer of Exod 12:23 at the time of the first Passover in Egypt.

* * *

In addition to Num 17:6-15 in Judaic tradition, one other OT text may have been in the back of Paul's mind when he dictated 2 Cor 2:14-17.

Ezek 20:33-44 deals with the eschatological restoration of Israel. The Lord will bring the Israelites out from the (heathen) peoples and gather them from the countries to which they have been scattered (v 34). In the wilderness of the peoples (v 35) He will purge out "the rebels" (הַמֹּרְדִים) among them (v 38).[145] Three times (in vv 38, 42 and 44) it is stated: "You shall know that I am the Lord" - when He does this.

In Jerusalem, on the Temple Mount, God will then accept those gathered (20:40). The verse continues: "there I will seek your contributions / offerings, and the first-fruits of your sacred contributions / taxes, with all your sacred things." Verse 41 continues: "As a pleasing odor I will accept you when I bring you out from the peoples, and gather you out of the countries where you have been scattered...."

Paul may have understood the above Ezekiel text through his eschatological "Christian" eyes, applying it to his own collection enterprise. The Hebrew term רֵאשִׁית in v 40 is translated by ἀπαρχαί in the Septuagint, "first-fruits." "Sacred contributions / taxes" is the plural of the Hebrew מַשְׂאָה.[146] This noun is also found in 2 Chron 24:6 and 9, where it refers to the collection of the half-sheqel "tax" required of every male Israelite and later Jew as of the age of twenty, also in the diaspora, including the Jews of Corinth.[147] The latter tax provided part of the background for Paul's collection of contributions for the poor saints in Jerusalem and Judea.[148] Ezek 20:41 has the expression רֵיחַ נִיחֹחַ, as explained before meaning "a pleasing odor," for which the LXX has ὀσμὴ εὐωδίας, exactly the expression Paul employs in Phil 4:18 regarding gifts received from the Philippians. Here in Philippians he may echo this verse from Ezekiel. The nouns ὀσμή and εὐωδία are employed by the Apostle separately, however, in 2 Cor 2:14-16.[149]

---

[145] The LXX has a different term here: τοὺς ἀσεβεῖς.
[146] Cf. BDB 673, 4. d.
[147] Cf. Exod 30:11-16 and the Mishnah tractate "Sheqelim."
[148] Cf. Philo, *Spec. Leg.* 1.77-78; *Leg. Gai.* 216, 311-16; Josephus, *Ant.* 18.310-13; and Nickle, *The Collection* 83.
[149] For this reason I agree with Alfred Plummer in his *Second Epistle of St Paul to the Corinthians* 71: "the sacrificial phrase ὀσμὴ εὐωδίας, so frequent in LXX, is not used here, and this makes any allusion to sacrifice doubtful." The primary

Nevertheless, it is possible that he was also encouraged to use them because of Ezek 20:41, in a context mentioning rebellion in the wilderness, just as in Num 17:6-15. This Ezekiel context was also eschatological, including the pilgrimage to Jerusalem of "first-fruits," thought of by Paul as his first converts.[150] In addition, the noun γνῶσις, "knowledge," and φανερόω, "to make known,"[151] in 2 Cor 2:14 may also have been triggered in Paul's mind by the three-fold occurrence of the expression "and you shall 'know' that I am the Lord" in Ezek 20:38, 42 and 44 (MT ידע , LXX ἐπιγινώσκω).[152] God "makes known" the fragrance of the "knowledge" of Christ (objective genitive) through the missionary work of Paul and his co-workers in every place, i.e. in the entire Mediterranean area.[153]

---

echo is rather of the sweet-smelling incense of Num 17:11-12 in Judaic tradition. On the non-sacrificial meaning, see also Christian Wolff in "Die *Paralipomena Jeremiae* und das Neue Testament" in *NTS* 51 (2005) 135, n. 97.

[150] Cf. again my art. "Paul's Travel Plans to Spain and the 'Full Number of the Gentiles' of Rom. XI 25" in *NovT* 21 (1979) 232-62. Ezek 20:41 is noted as one of several OT passages by R. Strachen, *The Second Epistle of Paul to the Corinthians* 75, and Ralph Martin, *2 Corinthians* 48. Regina Plunkett-Dowling also briefly notes LXX Ezek 20:40-41 in her *Reading and Restoration* 48-49, yet strangely maintains that Paul "quotes" it in 6:17. At the most (and I doubt it), there is an "echo" of it there, yet not a clear allusion.

[151] BAGD 852: reveal, make known, show.

[152] A connection to the larger Korah narrative may have been made here by Paul via the term "to make known" in Num 16:5 and "you shall know" in vv 28 and 30.

[153] For another example in Second Corinthians of Paul's combining Greco-Roman and Judaic traditions, cf. 4:16–5:10 and the brief comments on this section by John Fitzgerald in *The HarperCollins Study Bible*, ed. Wayne Meeks (New York: HarperCollins Publishers, 1993) 2171.

Summary

Somewhere in Macedonia the Apostle Paul wrote Second Corinthians or the individual sections which were later put together to form the present epistle. The catchword "Macedonia" (twice in 1:16, once in 2:13) caused him, a Roman citizen, to think of his namesake the Roman consul and general Paulus' well-known victory over the Macedonians in 168 BCE. It culminated in his brilliant and long-remembered triumphal procession through Rome for three days, November 27-29, 167 BCE. Aware of it and at least of some other occasions of *triumphus* / θρίαμβος , *triumphare* / θριαμβεύειν , including the *ovatio*, in the period just before his writing Second Corinthians, such as 17, 40, 43 and 47 CE, Paul in 2 Cor 2:14 thought of God as the Lord of "hosts" / "armies," a term he himself employs in Rom 9:29. It is this God to whom "thanks" (χάρις) are to be given when He leads Paul and his fellow missionaries in a triumphal procession (θριαμβεύοντι). The Roman Senate declared an official period of thanksgiving (*supplicatio*) upon receiving news of a general's major victory on the battlefield over an enemy. In addition, when he returned to Rome and was granted a triumph, the general's procession ended at the Temple of Jupiter, the main Roman god , on the Capitol. There the triumphator made offerings of thanksgiving for the god's (gods') help in procuring the victory.

Great amounts of incense, combined with wine to give it an even more fragrant odor, were employed in these offerings. While incense was also carried in the triumphal procession and utilized in the city's temples, opened for this special occasion, much greater amounts were used in the offerings of thanksgiving. The Roman custom of giving thanks in direct connection with a triumph explains how Paul could naturally employ "thanks be to God" in connection with triumphing in 2 Cor 2:14, just after the mention of Macedonia in v 13. There is thus no abrupt change in subject or style here, as proposed so often, and v 14 rightfully follows v 13. The custom also provided the Apostle with *one* major source for his expressions "fragrance" (ὀσμή) and "aroma" (εὐωδία) in vv 14-16.

The word "always" (πάντοτε) in 2:14 could very well be a slap on the part of Paul at the official state ideology of the Roman emperor as the "eternal triumphator." Victory does not "always" belong to the current head of state, who, as was well-known, usurped it from his own generals on the battlefield. Instead, it belongs only to God, who through the Resurrection of His Son Jesus Christ from the dead "conquered" the powers of sin and death once and for all (1 Cor 15:54-57).

Elsewhere in Second Corinthians Paul also employs imagery of warfare (6:7 and 10:3-4; cf. 1 Thess 5:8), and in Phil 2:25 and Phlm 2 he names two of his "fellow soldiers." The martial imagery of God, the Lord of "hosts'" "triumphing" in 2 Cor 2:14, however, does not portray Paul as a captured enemy general or king, who was led in chains and usually grimly executed at the end of the triumphal procession. Nor does it depict the Apostle here as a slave / servant. Rather, Paul and his fellow missionaries (Timothy and Silvanus) are depicted as the triumphator's officers, who walked behind or rode beside him in his triumphal procession. Paul employed a relatively infrequent, yet attested usage of θριαμβεύω here and used it metaphorically, just as at least five other writers of about his time also used the term "to triumph" in a metaphorical sense. This relatively infrequent meaning, which may be reflected in Augustine's translation of 2:14 as *triumphare nos facit* ("He makes / causes us to triumph") in his "Predestination of the Saints" 20,41, also fits the positive mood of the passage very well: Paul thanks God for always leading him and his co-workers in a triumphal procession, and for making known through them in every place the fragrance of the knowledge of Christ. Finally, Paul may well have had another form of the triumph in mind here, the *ovatio*, also translated as a verb (*ovo*) into Greek as θριαμβεύω. One form of the *ovatio* was awarded for gaining a major military victory, not by killing at least 5000 enemy soldiers, but by persuasion (πείθω). This is exactly what Paul and his missionary helpers did in their proclamation of the Gospel (5:11; 10:4-5). Pliny also notes in his *Natural History* 15,19 that the plural *ovantes* could include not only the triumphing general, but also his cavalrymen. That is, *they triumph with him*, just as Paul and his co-workers are portrayed as being led by God, the Lord of hosts, in His triumphal procession and as triumphing with Him. Livy in 7.13,10 has an example of soldiers entering Rome with their general, also described as their *triumphantes*, triumphing with him. There is a similar passage with θριαμβεύω in Appian, *The Civil Wars* 2,93.

Other aspects of the Roman general Paulus' military victory over Macedonia, his restructuring the province, and his triumphal procession may (in addition to other factors) have influenced Paul's thought elsewhere in Second Corinthians: the erection of centers for the collection of money for the poor saints in Jerusalem and Judea; the suspicion of fiscal impropriety; the mention of his family pedigree, boasting and weakness; consolation; and not working in another's missionary province.

The second major source of Paul's imagery in 2 Cor 2:14-17 was triggered by rebellion. Not only an individual rebelled against his apostolic authority (2:5-11; 7:12). So-called "super-apostles" later moved in and incited the Christian Corinthians against him (4:2 and thus 2:17; 10:10; 11:5-6; 12:16-18). This rebellion against the authority given him by the Lord (10:8; 13:10) caused Paul to think here of one of the most famous rebellions in the Hebrew Bible and the LXX, that of Korah and his followers, especially as found in Num 17:6-15 (Eng. 16:41-50). Judaic tradition on these verses, dealing with the congregation of the Israelites rebelling against Moses and Aaron, had already provided the Apostle with the image of the "Destroyer" in his first letter to the Corinthians (10:10). It now suggested other terminology to him in 2 Cor 2:14-17: incense, producing "fragrance" and "aroma" (reinforcing similar imagery from the triumphal procession); "those who are being saved" and "those who are perishing"; and "being sufficient," often considered puzzling in the present context.

Aaron, acting on the authority of Moses, here in Judaic tradition on Num 17:6-15 erects with his censer and the incense on it a partition between the dying and the living so that the Angel of Death, also labeled the Destroyer, cannot touch the living. As applied by Aaron at Moses' command, the sweet-smelling or fragrant incense leads to the Israelites' being "saved." In 2 Cor 2:14-16 the "fragrance" that comes from knowing Christ, also labeled the "aroma" of Christ to God, is incorporated by Paul and his co-workers. It is they who in their proclamation of the Gospel then stand like Aaron between life and death. The latter fate depends on how the Corinthians (and others) respond to this fragrance / aroma: positively, leading to life (in Christ), or negatively, leading to death. It is the Corinthians themselves who must now react to Paul and his fellow missionaries, those who speak as persons of sincerity (and authority), who stand in God's presence. They stand in contrast to those who are inciting rebellion in Corinth, who "peddle" God's word, the super-apostles.

Finally, Paul may also have had in mind here Ezek 20:40-41, also in a context of rebellion, influencing the choice of his expressions "knowledge" and "making known" in 2 Cor 2:14.

Summary

*   *   *

Paul's use of imagery in 2 Cor 2:14-17 primarily from the well-known custom of the Roman triumph, and from Judaic tradition on the notorious rebellion of Num 17:6-15, shows in an exemplary manner that although he had become a Christian, he also remained a Hellenistic Jew. He combined in his own person not only a major acquaintance with the Greco-Roman world, including its military conventions, but also a profound knowledge of his own Jewish heritage, both in Greek (the Septuagint) and in Hebrew / Aramaic (the Hebrew Bible, the targums in an earlier form, and Judaic tradition). There were very few, if any, who could match him in this regard, which still today makes him a fascinating figure for both Jews and Christians.

Sources and Reference Works

I. The Bible

Kittel, *Biblia Hebraica*, ed. R. Kittel et al. (Stuttgart: Privilegierte Württembergische Bibelanstalt, 1951[7]).

Rahlfs, *Septuaginta*, ed. A. Rahlfs (Stuttgart: Württembergische Bibelanstalt, 1962[7]).

Numeri, ed. J. Wevers (Septuaginta III,1; Göttingen: Vandenhoeck & Ruprecht, 1982).

Hatch-Redpath, *A Concordance to the Septuagint*, ed. E. Hatch and H. Redpath (Oxford: Clarendon Press, 1897; corrected reprint Grand Rapids, MI: Baker Book House, 1983), 2 vols.

Nestle / Aland, *Novum Testamentum Graece*, ed. E. Nestle, K. Aland, et al. (Stuttgart: Deutsche Bibelgesellschaft, 1990[26]).

The Greek New Testament, ed. B. Aland, K. Aland, J. Karavidopoulos, C. Martini and B. Metzger (Stuttgart: Deutsche Bibelgesellschaft, 2002[4]).

Hebrew New Testament, by F. Delitzsch (Berlin: Trowitzsch and Son, 1885).

Hebrew New Testament (Jerusalem: The United Bible Societies, 1979).

II. The Targums

Sperber, *The Bible in Aramaic*, ed. A. Sperber (Leiden: Brill, 1959), 4 vols.

Aberbach and Grossfeld, *Targum Onkelos to Genesis*, trans. M. Aberbach and B. Grossfeld (Denver: Center for Judaic Studies, University of Denver; New York: Ktav, 1982).

McNamara, *Targum Neofiti 1: Genesis*, trans. M. McNamara (The Aramaic Bible, 1A; Edinburgh: Clark, 1992).

Maher, *Targum Pseudo-Jonathan: Genesis*, trans. M. Maher (The Aramaic Bible, 1B; Edinburgh: Clark, 1992). *Exodus*, 1994.

Grossfeld, *The Targum Onqelos to Exodus*, trans. B. Grossfeld (The Aramaic Bible, 7; Edinburgh: Clark, 1988).

McNamara / Maher, *Targum Neofiti 1: Exodus, Targum Pseudo-Jonathan: Exodus*, trans. M. McNamara and M. Maher (The Aramaic Bible, 2: Edinburgh: Clark, 1994).
Grossfeld, *The Targum Onqelos to Leviticus, The Targum Onqelos to Numbers*, trans. B. Grossfeld (The Aramaic Bible, 8; Edinburgh: Clark, 1988).
McNamara / Maher, *Targum Neofiti 1: Leviticus, Targum Pseudo-Jonathan: Leviticus*, trans. M. McNamara and M. Maher (The Aramaic Bible, 3; Edinburgh: Clark, 1994).
McNamara / Maher, *Targum Neofiti 1: Numbers, Targum Pseudo-Jonathan: Numbers*, trans. M. McNamara and E. Clarke (The Aramaic Bible, 4; Edinburgh: Clark, 1995).
Clarke, *Targum Pseudo-Jonathan: Deuteronomy*, trans. E. Clarke (The Aramaic Bible, 5B; Edinburgh: Clark, 1998).
Rieder, *Targum Jonathan ben Uziel on the Pentateuch*, ed. with a Hebrew translation by D. Rieder (Jerusalem, 1984), 2 vols.
Díez Macho, *Neophyti 1*, ed. A. Díez Macho (Madrid: Consejo Superior de Investigaciones Científicas, 1968-78), 5 vols.
Klein, *The Fragment-Targums of the Pentateuch*, ed. and trans. M. Klein (AnBib 76; Rome: Biblical Institute, 1980), 2 vols.
Merino, *Targum de Salmos*, ed. L. Merino (Madrid: Consejo Superior de Investigaciones Científicas, 1984).
Stec, *The Targum of Psalms*, trans. D. Stec (The Aramaic Bible, 16; Collegeville, MN: Liturgical Press, 2004).

III. The Mishnah and Tosefta

Albeck, *Shisha Sidre Mishna*, ed. Ch. Albeck (Jerusalem and Tel Aviv: Bialik Institute and Dvir, 1975), 6 vols.
Danby, *The Mishnah*, trans. H. Danby (London: Oxford University Press, 1933).
Neusner, *The Mishnah*, trans. J. Neusner (New Haven: Yale University Press, 1988).
Zuckermandel, *Tosephta*, ed. M. Zuckermandel, with a supplement by S. Liebermann (Jerusalem: Wahrmann, 1970).
Neusner, *The Tosefta*, trans. J. Neusner et al. (Hoboken, NJ: KTAV, 1977-86), 6 vols.

IV. The Talmuds

Soncino, *The Babylonian Talmud*, ed. I. Epstein, various translators (London: Soncino, 1952), 18 vols. and index.
Soncino, *The Minor Tractates of the Talmud*, ed. A. Cohen, various translators (London: Soncino, 1965), 2 vols.
Goldschmidt, *Der Babylonische Talmud*, ed. with a German trans. by L. Goldschmidt (Haag: Nijoff, 1933), 9 vols.
Krotoshin, *Talmud Yerushalmi*, Krotoshin edition (Jerusalem: Shilah, 1969).
Neusner, *The Talmud of the Land of Israel*, trans. J. Neusner et al. (Chicago: University of Chicago Press, 1982-95), 34 vols.

V. Halakhic Midrashim

Lauterbach, *Mekilta de-Rabbi Ishmael*, ed. and trans. J. Lauterbach (Philadelphia: The Jewish Publication Society of America, 1976), 3 vols.
Epstein and Melamed, *Mekhilta d'Rabbi Sim'on b. Jochai*, ed. J. Epstein and E. Melamed (Jerusalem: Hillel Press, 1955; reprint 1979).
Finkelstein, *Sifre on Deuteronomy*, ed. L. Finkelstein (New York: The Jewish Theological Seminary of America, 1969).
Hammer, *Sifre*. A Tannaitic Commentary on the Book of Deuteronomy, trans. R. Hammer (YJS 24; New Haven: Yale University Press, 1986).
Neusner, *Sifre to Deuteronomy*. An Analytical Translation, trans. J. Neusner (BJS 98 and 101; Atlanta: Scholars Press, 1987), 2 vols.

VI. Haggadic Midrashim

Soncino, *Midrash Rabbah*, ed. H. Freedman and M. Simon (London: Soncino, 1939), 9 vols. and index.
Midrash Rabbah (Vilna: Romm, 1887).
Mirqin, *Midrash Rabbah*, Pentateuch. Ed. and vocalized by M. Mirqin (Tel Aviv: Yavneh, 1981), 11 vols.
Theodor and Albeck, *Midrash Bereshit Rabba*, ed. J. Theodor and Ch. Albeck (Jerusalem: Wahrmann, 1965), 3 vols.
Buber, *Midrasch Tanḥuma*: Ein agadischer Commentar zum Pentateuch, ed. S. Buber (Vilna: Romm, 1885).

Townsend, *Midrash Tanḥuma (S. Buber Recension)*, Vol. I, Genesis, Vol. II, Exodus and Leviticus, trans. J. Townsend (Hoboken, NJ: KTAV Publishing House, 1989 and 1997).

Midrash Tanḥuma, Eshkol edition (Jerusalem: Eshkol, no date), 2 vols.

Berman, *Midrash Tanhuma-Yelammedenu*. An English Translation of Genesis and Exodus...by S. Berman (Hoboken, NJ: KTAV Publishing House, 1996).

Friedmann, *Pesiqta Rabbati*, ed. M. Friedmann (Vienna, 1880; reprint Tel Aviv, 1962-63).

Braude, *Pesikta Rabbati*, trans. W. Braude (YJS 18; New Haven: Yale University Press, 1968), 2 vols.

Buber, *Midrasch Tehillim*, ed. S. Buber (Vilna: Romm, 1891).

Braude, *The Midrash on Psalms*, trans. W. Braude (YJS 13,1-2; New Haven: Yale University Press, 1959), 2 vols.

Eshkol, *Pirqe Rabbi Eliezer*, Eshkol edition (Jerusalem: Eshkol, 1973).

Friedlander, *Pirke de Rabbi Eliezer*, trans. G. Friedlander (New York: Hermon, 1970; original London, 1916).

Midrash Haggadol on the Pentateuch, ed. M. Margulies, A. Steinsalz, Z. Rabinowitz and S. Fisch (Jerusalem: Mosad Haraw Kook Publishing, 1975-76), 5 vols.

Guggenheimer, *Seder Olam*. The Rabbinic View of Biblical Chronology. Hebrew with English trans. by H. Guggenheimer (Northvale, NJ; Jerusalem: Jason Aronson, 1998).

Pentateuch with Targum Onkelos, Haphtaroth and Rashi's Commentary, Numbers, trans. M. Rosenbaum and A. Silberbaum (Jerusalem: The Silbermann Family, 1973).

VII. Apocrypha, Pseudepigrapha, Philo and Josephus

Apocrypha: see Rahlfs, *Septuaginta*.

OTP. *The Old Testament Pseudepigrapha*, ed. J. Charlesworth (Garden City, NY: Doubleday, 1983-85), 2 vols.

Philo, Greek and English trans. by F. Colson, G. Whitaker, J. Earp and R. Marcus (LCL; Cambridge, MA: Harvard University Press, 1921 / 1971), 10 vols. with 2 supplements.

The Philo Index, ed. P. Borgen, K. Fuglseth and R. Skarsten (Grand Rapids, MI: Eerdmans, 2000).

Josephus, Greek and English trans. by H. Thackeray, R. Marcus and A. Wikgren (LCL; Cambridge, MA: Harvard University Press, 1927 / 1969), 9 vols.

The Complete Concordance to Flavius Josephus. Study Edition, Supplemented by *Namenwörterbuch zu Flavius Josephus* by A. Schalit, ed. K. Rengsdorf (Leiden: Brill, 2002), 2 vols.

VIII. The Early Church, and Greek and Latin Pagan Authors

Ancient Christian Commentary on Scripture, New Testament VII, 1-2 Corinthians, ed. G. Bray (Downers Grove, IL: InterVarsity Press, 1999).
Aurelius Augustinus. Schriften gegen die Semipelagianer, Vol. VII, with "Die Vorherbestimmung der Heiligen," Latin and German trans. by A. Zumkeller (Würzburg: Augustinus-Verlag, 1987²).
Isidori Hispalensis Episcopi, *Etymologiarum sive Originum,* ed. W. Lindsay (Oxford: Clarendon Press, 1911).
Orose, *Histoires (Contre les Païens),* Latin and French trans. by M.-P. Arnaud-Lindet (Paris: Les belles Lettres, 1990), 3 vols.
Paulus Orosius, *Die antike Weltgeschichte in christlicher Sicht,* intro. C. Andresen with German trans. by A. Lippold (Zurich and Munich: Artemis Verlag, 1985-86), 2 vols.

* * *

Appian, *Roman History,* trans. H. White (LCL; Cambridge, MA: Harvard University Press, 1912 / 1990), 4 vols.
Athenaeus, *The Deipnosophists,* trans. C. Gulick (LCL; Cambridge, MA: Harvard University Press, 1927 / 1961), 7 vols.
Dio Cassius, *Roman History,* trans. E. Cary (LCL; Cambridge, MA: Harvard University Press, 1914 / 2001), 9 vols.
Diodorus of Sicily, *Library of History,* trans. C. Oldfather and F. Walton (LCL; Cambridge, MA: Harvard University Press, 1935 / 1961).
Dionysius of Halicarnassus, *Roman Antiquities,* trans. E. Cary (LCL; Cambridge, MA: Harvard University Press, 1937 / 1948), 7 vols.
Epictetus, trans. W. Oldfather (LCL; Cambridge, MA: Harvard University Press, 1928 / 1959), 2 vols.
Pausanias, *Description of Greece,* trans. W. Jones (LCL; Cambridge, MA: Harvard University Press, 1918 / 1954).
Plutarch, *Parallel Lives of Greeks and Romans,* trans. B. Perrin (LCL; Cambridge, MA: Harvard University Press, 1914 / 1982), 11 vols.
Polybius, *Histories,* trans. W. Paton (LCL; Cambridge, MA: Harvard University Press, 1922 / 2000), 6 vols.

M. IVNIANI IVSTINI EPITOMA HISTORIARUM PHILIPPICARUM POMPEI TROGI, ed. O. Seel (Stuttgart: Teubner, 1985).
Pompeius Trogus, *Weltgeschichte von den Anfängen bis Augustus, im Auszug des Justin*, German trans. by O. Seel (Zurich / Munich: Artemis Verlag, 1972).
Theophrastus, *Enquiry into Plants, and Minor Works on Odours and Weather Signs*, trans. A. Hort (LCL; Cambridge, MA: Harvard University Press, 1916 / 1961), 2 vols.
Theophrastus, *De odoribus*, ed. U. Eigler and G. Wöhrle (Beiträge zur Altertumskunde 37; Stuttgart: Teubner, 1993).

* * *

Apuleius, *Metamorphoses*, trans. J. Hanson (LCL; Cambridge, MA: Harvard University Press, 1989), 2 vols.
Cicero, *In Catilinam I-IV – Pro Murena – Pro Sulla – Pro Flacco*, trans. L. Lord (LCL; Cambridge, MA: Harvard University Press, 1937 / 1967).
Epistolae ad Familiares, Libri I-XVI, ed. D. Shackleton Bailey (Stuttgart: Teubner, 1988).
Pro T. Annio Milone – In L. Calpurnium Pisonem, etc., trans. N. Watts (LCL; Cambridge, MA: Harvard University Press, 1931 / 1972).
The Speeches, with "Pro Cluentio," trans. H. Grose Hodge (LCL; Cambridge, MA: Harvard University Press, 1927 / 1966).
Tusculan Disputations, trans. J. King (LCL; Cambridge, MA: Harvard University Press, 1927 / 1971).
Florus, *Epitome of Roman History*, trans. E. Forster (LCL; Cambridge, MA: Harvard University Press, 1929 / 1995).
Gellius, *The Attic Nights of Aulus Gellius*, trans. J. Rolfe (LCL; Cambridge, MA: Harvard University Press, 1927 / 1961), 3 vols.
Horace, *The Odes and Epodes*, trans. C. Bennett (LCL; Cambridge, MA: Harvard University Press, 1914 / 1968).
Juvenal and Perseus, including the Satires of Juvenal, trans. G. Ramsay (LCL; Cambridge, MA: Harvard University Press, 1920 / 1950).
Livy, *History of Rome*, trans. B. Foster, F. Moore, E. Sage and A. Schlesinger (LCL; Cambridge, MA: Harvard University Press, 1919 / 2004), 14 vols.
Ovid, *The Art of Love and Other Poems*, trans. J. Mozley (LCL; Cambridge, MA: Harvard University Press, 1929 / 1979).
Fasti, trans. J. Frazer (1931 / 1959).
Heroides. Amores, trans. G. Showerman and G. Goold (1977 / 1996).
Metamorphoses, trans. F. Miller and G. Goold (1984), 2 vols.

Tristia, trans. A. Wheeler (1924 / 1959).
Pliny, *Natural History*, trans. H. Rackham, W. Jones and D. Eichholz (LCL; Cambridge, MA: Harvard University Press, 1938 / 1962), 10 vols.
Seneca, *Moral Essays*, trans. J. Basore (LCL; Cambridge, MA: Harvard University Press, 1932 / 1958), 3 vols., with "De Vita Beata" in vol. 2, and "De Beneficiis" in vol. 3.
Sexti Pompei Festi, *De verborum significatu quae supersunt cum Pauli epitome*, ed. W. Lindsay (Stuttgart / Leipzig: Teubner, 1913 / 1997).
Suetonius, *The Lives of the Caesars*, trans. J. Rolfe (LCL; Cambridge, MA: Harvard University Press, 1913 / 1989), 2 vols.
Tacitus, *The Annals*, trans. J. Jackson (LCL; Cambridge, MA: Harvard University Press, 1931 / 1969), 3 vols.
Valerius Maximus, *Memorable Doings and Sayings*, trans. D. Shackleton Bailey (LCL; Cambridge, MA: Harvard University Press, 2000), 2 vols.
Velleius Paterculus, *Compendium of Roman History*, trans. F. Shipley (LCL; Cambridge, MA: Harvard University Press, 1924 / 1961).

IX. Dictionaries and Reference Works

BDB, *A Hebrew and English Lexicon of the Old Testament*, by F. Brown, S. Driver and C. Briggs (Oxford: Clarendon Press, 1962).
Jastrow, *A Dictionary of the Targumim, the Talmud Babli and Yerushalmi, and the Midrashic Literature*, by M. Jastrow (New York: Pardes, 1950), 2 vols.
Hyman, *Torah Hakethubah Vehamessurah. A Reference Book of the Scriptural Passages Quoted in Talmudic, Midrashic and Early Rabbinic Literature*, by Aaron Hyman, second edition by Arthur Hyman (Tel Aviv: Dvir, 1979), 3 vols.
Ginzberg, *The Legends of the Jews*, by L. Ginzberg (Philadelphia: The Jewish Publication Society of America, 1968), 6 vols.
Str-B, *Kommentar zum Neuen Testament aus Talmud und Midrasch*, by (H. Strack and) P. Billerbeck (Munich: Beck, 1924-61), 6 vols.
Strack and Stemberger, *Introduction to the Talmud and Midrash*, by H. Strack and G. Stemberger (Minneapolis: Fortress Press, 1992).
Nickelsburg, *Jewish Literature Between the Bible and the Mishnah*, by G. Nickelsburg (Philadelphia: Fortress Press, 1981).
IDB, *The Interpreter's Dictionary of the Bible*, ed. G. Buttrick et al. (New York and Nashville: Abingdon Press, 1962), 4 vols. Supplementary Volume, ed. K. Crim, 1976.

TDNT, Theological Dictionary of the New Testament, ed. G. Kittel and G. Friedrich (Grand Rapids, MI: Eerdmans, 1964-76), 9 vols. and index.

EWNT, Exegetisches Wörterbuch zum Neuen Testament, ed. H. Balz and G. Schneider (Stuttgart: Kohlhammer, 1992²).

TWAT, Theologisches Wörterbuch zum Alten Testament, ed. G. Botterweck and H. Ringgren (Stuttgart: Kohlhammer, 1973-2000), 10 vols.

LSJ, *A Greek-English Lexicon*, by H. Liddell, R. Scott and H. Jones (Oxford: Clarendon Press, 1966⁹).

BAGD, *A Greek-English Lexicon of the New Testament and Other Early Christian Literature*, by W. Bauer, W. Arndt, F. Gingrich and F. Danker (Chicago: University of Chicago Press, 1979²).

Lampe, *A Patristic Greek Lexicon*, by G. Lampe (Oxford: Clarendon Press, 1961 / 1991).

PW, *Realencyclopädie der classischen Altertumswissenschaft*, ed. A. Pauly, G. Wissowa et al. (Stuttgart: Metzler, 1889-).

KP, *Der kleine Pauly*, ed. K. Ziegler and W. Sontheimer (Stuttgart: Alfred Druckenmüller, 1964-75), 5 vols.

Der neue Pauly, ed. H. Cancik and H. Schneider (Stuttgart / Weimar: Metzler, 1996-2003), 16 vols.

The Oxford Classical Dictionary, ed. N. Hammond and H. Scullard (Oxford: Clarendon Press, 1970²).

The Oxford Companion to Classical Literature, ed. M. Howatson (Oxford: Oxford University Press, 1989²).

Aufstieg und Niedergang der römischen Welt, ed. H. Temporini and W. Haase (Berlin: de Gruyter, 1972-96), 37 in part multiple vols.

Oxford Latin Dictionary, ed. P. Glare (Oxford: Clarendon Press, 1996).

Chambers Murray, latin-english Dictionary, ed. W. Smith and J. Lockwood (Edinburgh: Chambers; London: Murray, 1986).

Author Index

Allo, E.-B. 71
Attridge, H. 62
Augustine 20, 43, 82
Aus, R. 9, 74, 79

Badian, E. 1
Barnett, P. 40, 71
Barrett, C. 20, 27, 29, 40, 72
Basore, J. 22
Betz, H. ....ix, 42
Beza 43
Billerbeck, P. (Str-B) 56, 68, 76
Bjerkelund, C. 33
Börner, F. 2, 14
Bornkamm, G. 42, 45
Breytenbach, C. ....vii, 18,
....22-23, 43-44
Bruce, F. 20, 44
Bultmann, R. 31, 41, 44

Calvin, J. 20
Collange, J.-F. 41-42, 71
Colson, F. 58

Dautzenberg, G. 1, 44
Decker, W. 1
Delling, G. 1, 73
Duff, P. 40, 42-43, 45

Eder, W. 3
Egan, R. 44
Ehlers, W. 1, 37
Eissfeldt, O. 52
Elvers, K.-L. 5

Field, F. 42, 44
Findlay, G. 42
Fitzgerald, J. ....vii, 9, 79
Fraenkel, E. 13
Furnish, V. 42, 44

Georgi, D. 45, 71
Ginzberg, L. 53, 75
Gizewski, C. 36
Goodenough, E. 57
Grant, M. 17-18
Gruber, M. 40, 42-44, 62
Gundel, H. 5

Hadas, M. 59
Hafemann, S. 43
Halkin, L. 9-11
Halpern, D. 65
Hays, R. 49
Héring, J. 20
Holloway, P. 35

Ibrahim, L. 15

Jastrow, M. 51, 53, 65
Jones, P. 71

Kern, O. 38
Kinsey, A. 42-43
Klauck, H.-J. 15, 40, 43
Klebs, E. 5
Kötting, B. 73
Kremer, J. 75
Krenz, E. 1

Kügler, J. ....ix, 43
Kümmel, W. 20
Künzl, E. 1-3, 5, 8, 12-13, 36
Kuhnert, E. 38

Lambrecht, J. 44, 71
Lang, F. 75
Larcher, C. 52-53
Levine, B. 51
Lieberman, S. 5
Lierman, J. 48
Lietzmann, H. 44, 71
Lohmeyer, E. 73

Malherbe, A. 17, 35
Manson, T. 41, 68
Marshall, P. 21, 44
Martin, R. 41-42, 79
Mc Cormick, M. 1, 8
Meeks, W. ....vii, 74
Meyer, H. 75, 77
Müller, W. 12

Nickelsburg, G. 53, 59
Nickle, K. 24, 78

Oswald, N. vii

Paton, W. 32
Perrin, B. 30
Plummer, A. 27, 40, 71,
....................................75, 78
Plunkett-Dowling, R. ......vii, ix,
...................................40, 46,
................................48, 68, 79
Pope, R. 45
Prescendi, F. 38

Rashi 65, 67
Reider, J. 53, 56
Reiter, W. 5, 30
Rengstorf, K. 71
Robertson, A. 75

Rohde, G. 36-37
Rylaarsdam, J. 25

Schäfer, P. 60, 65
Schlesinger, A. 10
Schmitz, O. 33
Schneider, J. 76
Schön, G. 5
Schröter, J. 43
Schwenk-Bressler, U. 53-54
Scott, J. 45, 65
Scranton, R. 15
Senft, C. 75
Shaw, J. 15
Siebert, A. 9, 11
Stählin, G. 33
Stemberger, G. 5
Strachen, R. 44, 71, 79
Strack, H. 5
Stumpff, A. 73

Thrall, M. 40-41, 71

Versnel, H. 1, 36

Walbank, W. 14
Wallisch, E. 4
Webster, G. 17-18
Weiss, J. 75
Wendland, H.-D. 20, 40
Wettstein, J. 68
Whitaker, G. 58
Williamson, Jr., L. 41, 45
Windisch, H. 20, 40, 71
Winston, D. 53
Wiseman, J. 14
Wöhrle, G. 12
Wolff, C. 75, 79

Zeller, D. vii
Zobel, H.-J. 16

About the Author

Roger David Aus, b. 1940, studied English and German at St. Olaf College, and theology at Harvard Divinity School, Luther Theological Seminary, and Yale University, from which he received the Ph.D. degree in New Testament Studies in 1971. He is an ordained clergyman of the Evangelical Lutheran Church in America, and pastor emeritus of the German-speaking Luthergemeinde in Berlin-Reinickendorf, Germany. The Protestant Church of Berlin-Brandenburg (Berlin West) kindly granted him a short study leave in Jerusalem, Israel, in 1981. His study of New Testament topics always reflects his great interest in, and deep appreciation of, the Jewish roots of the Christian faith.

Other volumes by Roger David Aus

Matthew 1-2 and the Virginal Conception In Light of Palestinian and Hellenistic Judaic Traditions on the Birth of Israel's First Redeemer, Moses (Studies in Judaism; Lanham, MD: University Press of America, 2004).

My Name Is "Legion." Palestinian Judaic Traditions in Mark 5:1-20 and Other Gospel Texts (Studies in Judaism; Lanham, MD: University Press of America, 2003).

The Stilling of the Storm. Studies in Early Palestinian Judaic Traditions (International Studies in Formative Christianity and Judaism; Binghamton, NY: Global Publications, Binghamton University, 2000). Essays on Mark 4:35-41; 1:16-20; and Luke 24:13-35.

"Caught in the Act," Walking on the Sea, and the Release of Barabbas Revisited (South Florida Studies in the History of Judaism, 157; Atlanta: Scholars Press, 1998). Essays on John 7:53 - 8:11; Mark 6:45-52 par.; and 15:6-15 par.

The Wicked Tenants and Gethsemane (International Studies in Formative Christianity and Judaism, University of South Florida, 4; Atlanta: Scholars Press, 1996). Essays on Mark 12:1-9 par.; 14:32-42 par.; 2 Cor 12:1-10; and Judas' handing Jesus over to certain death through a kiss.

Samuel, Saul and Jesus. Three Early Palestinian Jewish Christian Gospel Haggadoth (South Florida Studies in the History of Judaism, 105; Atlanta: Scholars Press, 1994). Essays on Luke 2:41-51a; Mark 6:1-6a par.; and the prodigia at Jesus' crucifixion.

Barabbas and Esther and Other Studies in the Judaic Illumination of Earliest Christianity (South Florida Studies in the History of Judaism, 54; Atlanta: Scholars Press, 1992). Essays on Mark 15:6-15 par.; John 11:45-54; Luke 15:11-32; Matt 2:1-12; Gal 2:9; Isa 66:7, Revelation 12 and 2 Thessalonians 1; 2 Thess 2:6-7; Rom 11:25; and 2 Thess 1:3.

Weihnachtsgeschichte, Barmherziger Samariter, Verlorener Sohn. Studien zu ihrem jüdischen Hintergrund (ANTZ 2; Berlin: Institut Kirche und Judentum, 1988). Essays on Luke 2:1-20; 10:30-37; and 15:11-32.

Water into Wine and the Beheading of John the Baptist. Early Jewish-Christian Interpretation of Esther 1 in John 2:1-11 and Mark 6:17-29 (Brown Judaic Studies, 150; Atlanta: Scholars Press, 1988).

STUDIES IN JUDAISM
TITLES IN THE SERIES
PUBLISHED BY UNIVERSITY PRESS OF AMERICA

Judith Z. Abrams
The Babylonian Talmud: A Topical Guide, 2002.

Roger David Aus
Matthew 1-2 and the Virginal Conception: In Light of Palestinian and Hellenistic Judaic Traditions on the Birth of Israel's First Redeemer, Moses, 2004.

My Name Is "Legion": Palestinian Judaic Traditions in Mark 5:1-20 and Other Gospel Texts, 2003.

Alan L. Berger, Harry James Cargas, and Susan E. Nowak
The Continuing Agony: From the Carmelite Convent to the Crosses at Auschwitz, 2004.

S. Daniel Breslauer
Creating a Judaism without Religion: A Postmodern Jewish Possibility, 2001.

Bruce Chilton
Targumic Approaches to the Gospels: Essays in the Mutual Definition of Judaism and Christianity, 1986.

David Ellenson
Tradition in Transition: Orthodoxy, Halakhah, and the Boundaries of Modern Jewish Identity, 1989.

Paul V. M. Flesher
New Perspectives on Ancient Judaism, Volume 5: Society and Literature in Analysis, 1990.

Marvin Fox
Collected Essays on Philosophy and on Judaism, Volume One: Greek Philosophy, Maimonides, 2003.

Collected Essays on Philosophy and on Judaism, Volume Two: Some Philosophers, 2003.

Collected Essays on Philosophy and on Judaism, Volume Three: Ethics, Reflections, 2003.

Zev Garber
Methodology in the Academic Teaching of Judaism, 1986.

Zev Garber, Alan L. Berger, and Richard Libowitz
Methodology in the Academic Teaching of the Holocaust, 1988.

Abraham Gross
Spirituality and Law: Courting Martyrdom in Christianity and Judaism, 2005.

Harold S. Himmelfarb and Sergio DellaPergola
Jewish Education Worldwide: Cross-Cultural Perspectives, 1989.

William Kluback
The Idea of Humanity: Hermann Cohen's Legacy to Philosophy and Theology, 1987.

Samuel Morell
Studies in the Judicial Methodology of Rabbi David ibn Abi Zimra, 2004.

Jacob Neusner
The Aggadic Role in Halakhic Discourses: Volume I, 2001.

The Aggadic Role in Halakhic Discourses: Volume II, 2001.

The Aggadic Role in Halakhic Discourses: Volume III, 2001.

Analysis and Argumentation in Rabbinic Judaism, 2003.

Ancient Judaism and Modern Category-Formation: "Judaism," "Midrash," "Messianism," and Canon in the Past Quarter Century, 1986.

Canon and Connection: Intertextuality in Judaism, 1987.

Dual Discourse, Single Judaism, 2001.

The Emergence of Judaism: Jewish Religion in Response to the Critical Issues of the First Six Centuries, 2000.

First Principles of Systemic Analysis: The Case of Judaism within the History of Religion, 1988.

The Halakhah and the Aggadah, 2001.

Halakhic Hermeneutics, 2003.

The Hermeneutics of Rabbinic Category Formations, 2001.

How Not to Study Judaism, Examples and Counter-Examples, Volume One: Parables, Rabbinic Narratives, Rabbis' Biographies, Rabbis' Disputes, 2004.

How Not to Study Judaism, Examples and Counter-Examples, Volume Two: Ethnicity and Identity versus Culture and Religion, How Not to Write a Book on Judaism, Point and Counterpoint, 2004.

Is Scripture the Origin of the Halakhah? 2005.

Israel and Iran in Talmudic Times: A Political History, 1986.

Israel's Politics in Sasanian Iran: Self-Government in Talmudic Times, 1986.

Judaism in Monologue and Dialogue, 2005.

Major Trends in Formative Judaism, Fourth Series, 2002.

Major Trends in Formative Judaism, Fifth Series, 2002.

Messiah in Context: Israel's History and Destiny in Formative Judaism, 1988.

The Native Category - Formations of the Aggadah: The Later Midrash-Compilations - Volume I, 2000.

The Native Category - Formations of the Aggadah: The Earlier Midrash-Compilations - Volume II, 2000.

Paradigms in Passage: Patterns of Change in the Contemporary Study of Judaism, 1988.

Parsing the Torah, 2005.

The Religious Study of Judaism: Description, Analysis and Interpretation, Volume 1, 1986.

The Religious Study of Judaism: Description, Analysis, Interpretation, Volume 2, 1986.

The Religious Study of Judaism: Context, Text, Circumstance, Volume 3, 1987.

The Religious Study of Judaism: Description, Analysis, Interpretation, Volume 4: Ideas of History, Ethics, Ontology, and Religion in Formative Judaism, 1988.

Struggle for the Jewish Mind: Debates and Disputes on Judaism Then and Now, 1988.

The Talmud Law, Theology, Narrative: A Sourcebook, 2005.

Talmud Torah: Ways to God's Presence through Learning: An Exercise in Practical Theology, 2002.

Texts Without Boundaries: Protocols of Non-Documentary Writing in the Rabbinic Canon: Volume I: The Mishnah, Tractate Abot, and the Tosefta, 2002.

Texts Without Boundaries: Protocols of Non-Documentary Writing in the Rabbinic Canon: Volume II: Sifra and Sifré to Numbers, 2002.

Texts Without Boundaries: Protocols of Non-Documentary Writing in the Rabbinic Canon: Volume III: Sifré to Deuteronomy and Mekhilta Attributed to Rabbi Ishmael, 2002.

Texts Without Boundaries: Protocols of Non-Documentary Writing in the Rabbinic Canon: Volume IV: Leviticus Rabbah, 2002.

A Theological Commentary to the Midrash - Volume I: Pesiqta deRab Kahana, 2001.

A Theological Commentary to the Midrash - Volume II: Genesis Raba, 2001.

A Theological Commentary to the Midrash - Volume III: Song of Songs Rabbah, 2001.

A Theological Commentary to the Midrash - Volume IV: Leviticus Rabbah, 2001.

A Theological Commentary to the Midrash - Volume V: Lamentations Rabbati, 2001.

A Theological Commentary to the Midrash - Volume VI: Ruth Rabbah and Esther Rabbah, 2001.

A Theological Commentary to the Midrash - Volume VII: Sifra, 2001.

A Theological Commentary to the Midrash - Volume VIII: Sifré to Numbers and Sifré to Deuteronomy, 2001.

A Theological Commentary to the Midrash - Volume IX: Mekhilta Attributed to Rabbi Ishmael, 2001.

Theological Dictionary of Rabbinic Judaism: Part One: Principal Theological Categories, 2005.

Theological Dictionary of Rabbinic Judaism: Part Two: Making Connections and Building Constructions, 2005.

Theological Dictionary of Rabbinic Judaism: Part Three: Models of Analysis, Explanation, and Anticipation, 2005.

Theology of Normative Judaism: A Source Book, 2005.

The Torah and the Halakhah: The Four Relationships, 2003.

The Unity of Rabbinic Discourse: Volume I: Aggadah in the Halakhah, 2001.

The Unity of Rabbinic Discourse: Volume II: Halakhah in the Aggadah, 2001.

The Unity of Rabbinic Discourse: Volume III: Halakhah and Aggadah in Concert, 2001.

The Vitality of Rabbinic Imagination: The Mishnah Against the Bible and Qumran, 2005.

Who, Where and What is "Israel?": Zionist Perspectives on Israeli and American Judaism, 1989.

The Wonder-Working Lawyers of Talmudic Babylonia: The Theory and Practice of Judaism in its Formative Age, 1987.

Jacob Neusner and Ernest S. Frerichs
New Perspectives on Ancient Judaism, Volume 2: Judaic and Christian Interpretation of Texts: Contents and Contexts, 1987.

New Perspectives on Ancient Judaism, Volume 3: Judaic and Christian Interpretation of Texts: Contents and Contexts, 1987.

Jacob Neusner and James F. Strange
Religious Texts and Material Contexts, 2001.

David Novak and Norbert M. Samuelson
Creation and the End of Days: Judaism and Scientific Cosmology, 1986.

Proceedings of the Academy for Jewish Philosophy, 1990.

Aaron D. Panken
The Rhetoric of Innovation: Self-Conscious Legal Change in Rabbinic Literature, 2005.

Norbert M. Samuelson
Studies in Jewish Philosophy: Collected Essays of the Academy for Jewish Philosophy, 1980-1985, 1987.

Benjamin Edidin Scolnic
Alcimus, Enemy of the Maccabees, 2004.

If the Egyptians Drowned in the Red Sea Where are Pharaoh's Chariots?: Exploring the Historical Dimension of the Bible, 2005.

Rivka Ulmer
Pesiqta Rabbati: A Synoptic Edition of Pesiqta Rabbati Based upon all Extant Manuscripts and the Editio Princeps, Volume III, 2002.

Manfred H. Vogel
A Quest for a Theology of Judaism: The Divine, the Human and the Ethical Dimensions in the Structure-of-Faith of Judaism Essays in Constructive, 1987.

Anita Weiner
Renewal: Reconnecting Soviet Jewry to the Soviet People: A Decade of American Jewish Joint Distribution Committee (AJJDC) Activities in the Former Soviet Union 1988-1998, 2003.

Eugene Weiner and Anita Weiner
Israel-A Precarious Sanctuary: War, Death and the Jewish People, 1989.

The Martyr's Conviction: A Sociological Analysis, 2002.

Leslie S. Wilson
The Serpent Symbol in the Ancient Near East: Nahash and Asherah: Death, Life, and Healing, 2001.